One More Once Upon a Time

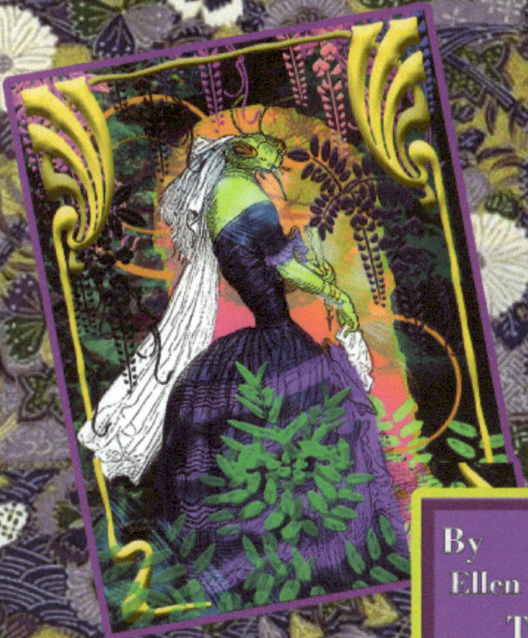

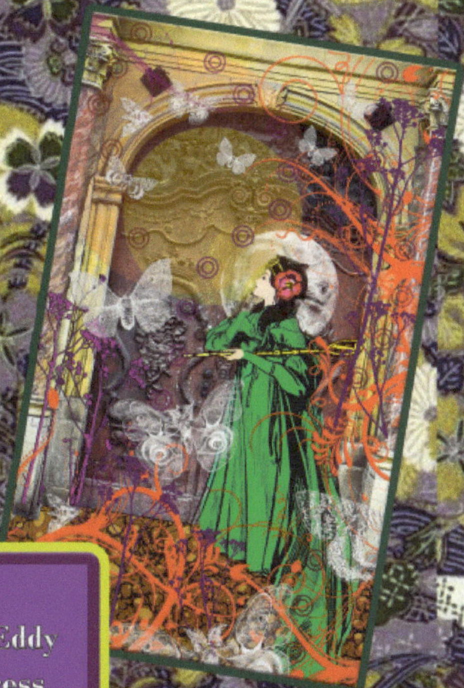

By
Ellen Anne Eddy
TMS Press

Acknowledgments:

The Illustrations of Niell, Neilsen, Denslow, Tenniel and Grandville are in the public domain and available at many different sites. These illustrations are from Project Gutenberg.

Dedication

To Lauren for her careful eye and endless help

And to Don who keeps my world quiet, stable and sweet.

One More Once Upon A Time
By Ellen Anne Eddy

Copyright 2018
ISBN 978-1-7322850-1-9
TMS Press
Galesburg, IL 61401

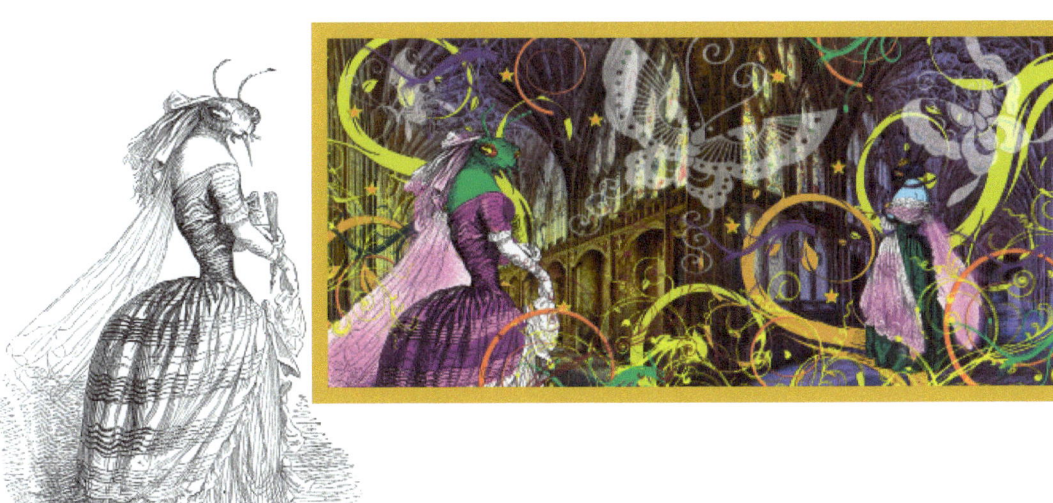

About this Book

I love the black and white illustrations from vintage children's books. But my sense of humor and imagination get the best of me, and I need to play with them a bit. This is a grouping of collages, done with Photoshop, featuring illustrations from Tenniel's *Alice in Wonderland,* Kay Nielsen, Frank Baum's *Wizard of Oz* series, and Grandville's *Les Animaux.*

Although these illustrations were drawn for other stories, they are archetypal images in every sense, part of our consciousness. They could illustrate a million different stories.

Flights of fancy fly!

Ellen Anne Eddy

Gilding the Lily

I've always loved coloring books. I've always loved rubber stamps, collage and pop-up books. One of the limits of my life is that I can't do any of those things without making an unholy mess. My kindergarten teacher was dismayed to report that I could not be trusted not to eat paste or run with scissors.

I also have a passion for early children's books' illustrations. Granville was hardly a child's book illustrator. His work was satire of adult issues in the French revolution. The first time I saw his illustrations my eyes blew open, my skirt flew up, and I was in love.

But I can't help myself. As glorious as they are, I want to color them, put them into collage and put titles on them. It's sort of like dressing paper dolls.

I could do none of those things physically. Photoshop with its endless fix-it factor and layers makes it possible.

They were also too fun not to share. So I will ask Grandville, Denslow, Neill, Neilsen, and Tenniel to forgive me for playing in their world. I couldn't help myself. I had to gild the lily.

I don't intend this book to be a how-to. I'll briefly go through how these images were produced, but anyone with a knowledge of Photoshop will instantly know. It's layer after layer of images and color and texture, made with images, overlays, and brushes. Strangely that's not at all different from what I did for years with fabric. With the delightful difference that being virtual, it can be changed endlessly until it's right.

As an aside it overlaid my imagination onto theirs. But that might be what was most wonderful about these illustrators. Not only did they open up the artist's imagination for us, they sent ours spinning further out there. This is where mine landed.

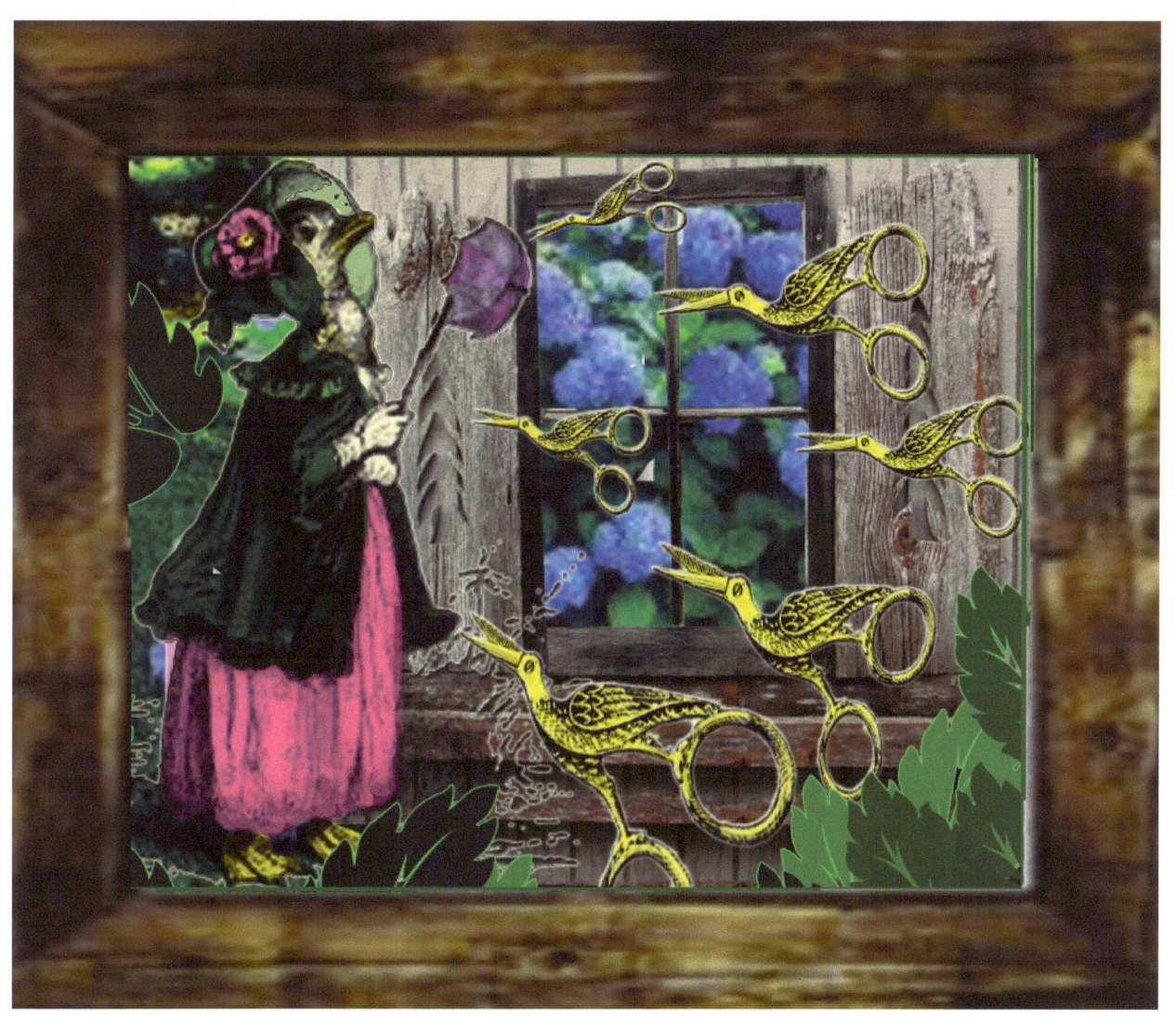

Conversations with Scissors

Normally I don't speak to storks, but since they came as a delegation....

Grandville

Grandville's *Les Animaux* described the French Revolution in period costumed animal images. The drawings are still fresh, funny and personal, each a story unto itself.

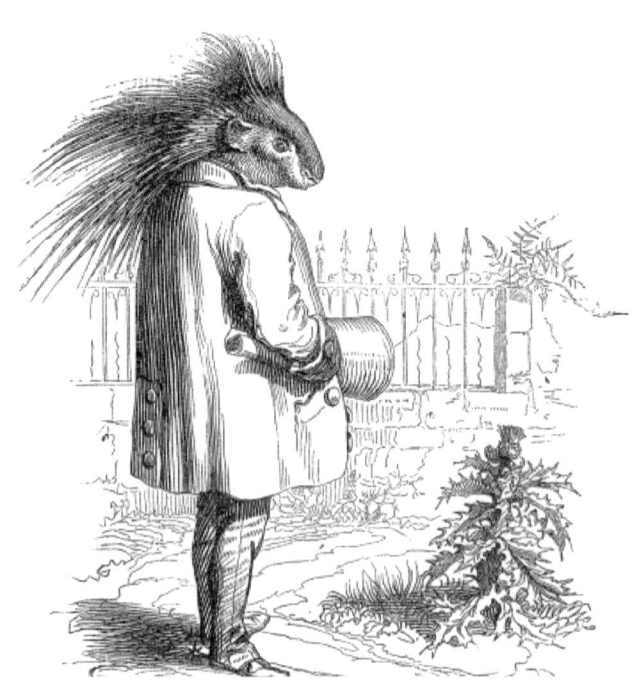

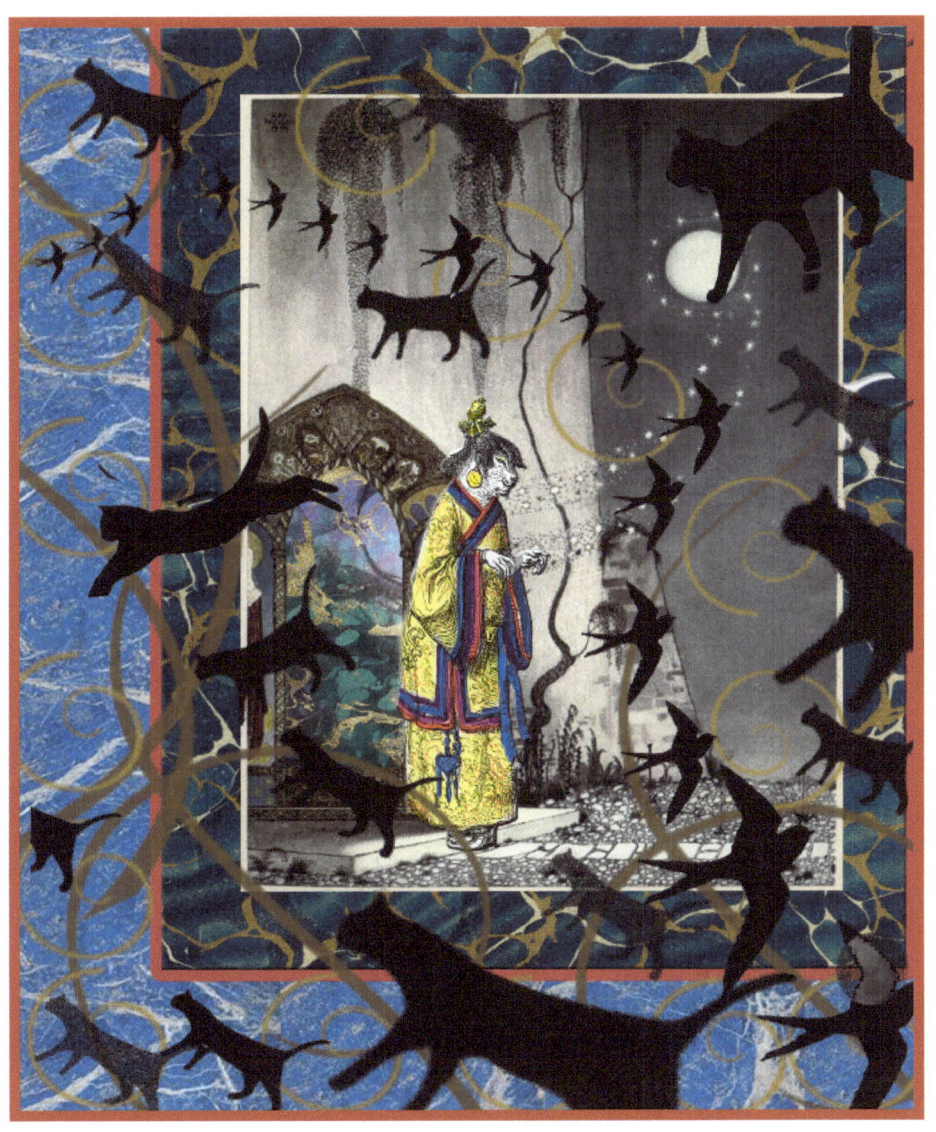

Cat Moon

My darlings hunt the night to search for the best mice, and pools of moonlight....

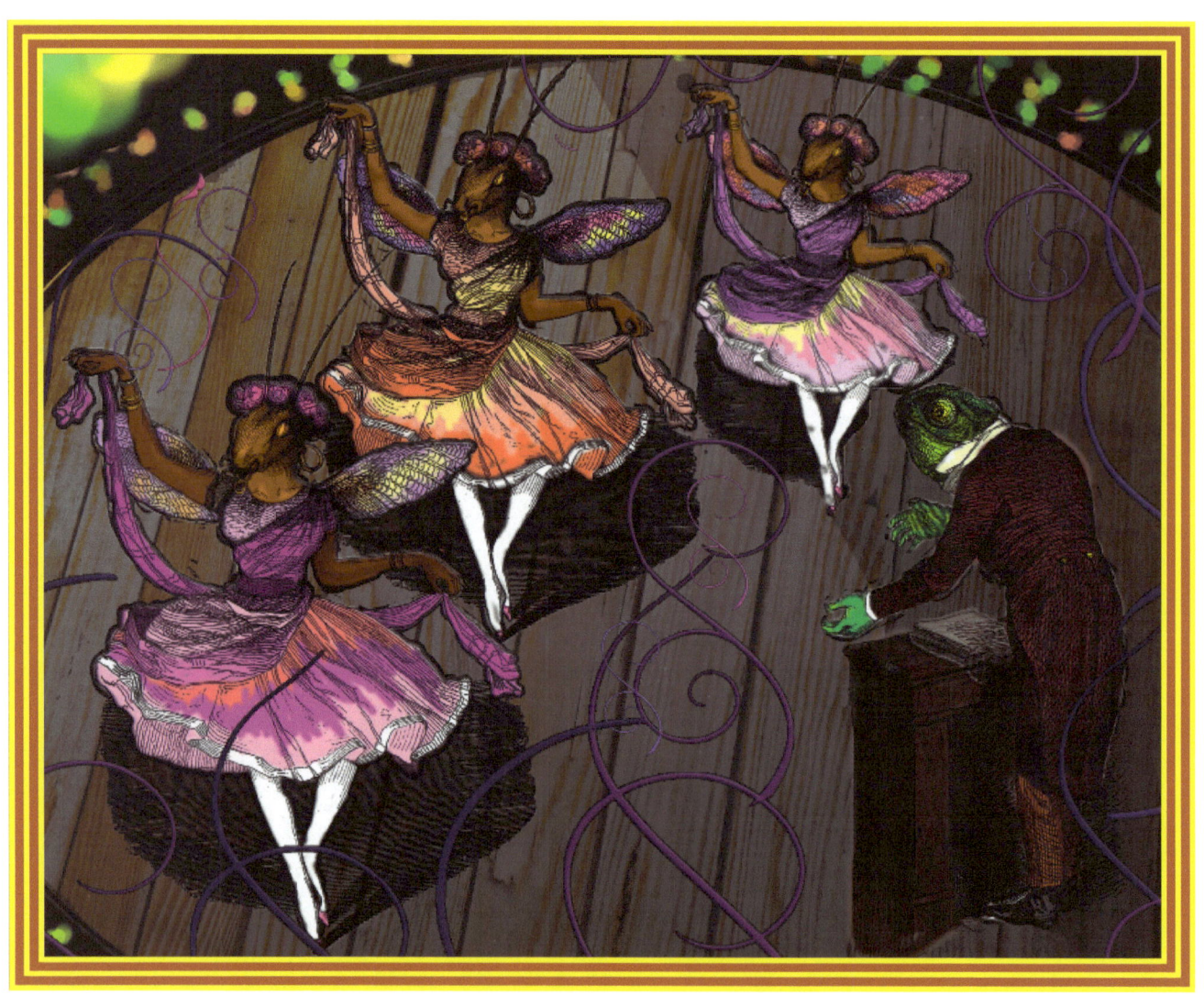

Limelight

Yes, for now I'm in the chorus line, but the maestro has noticed me....

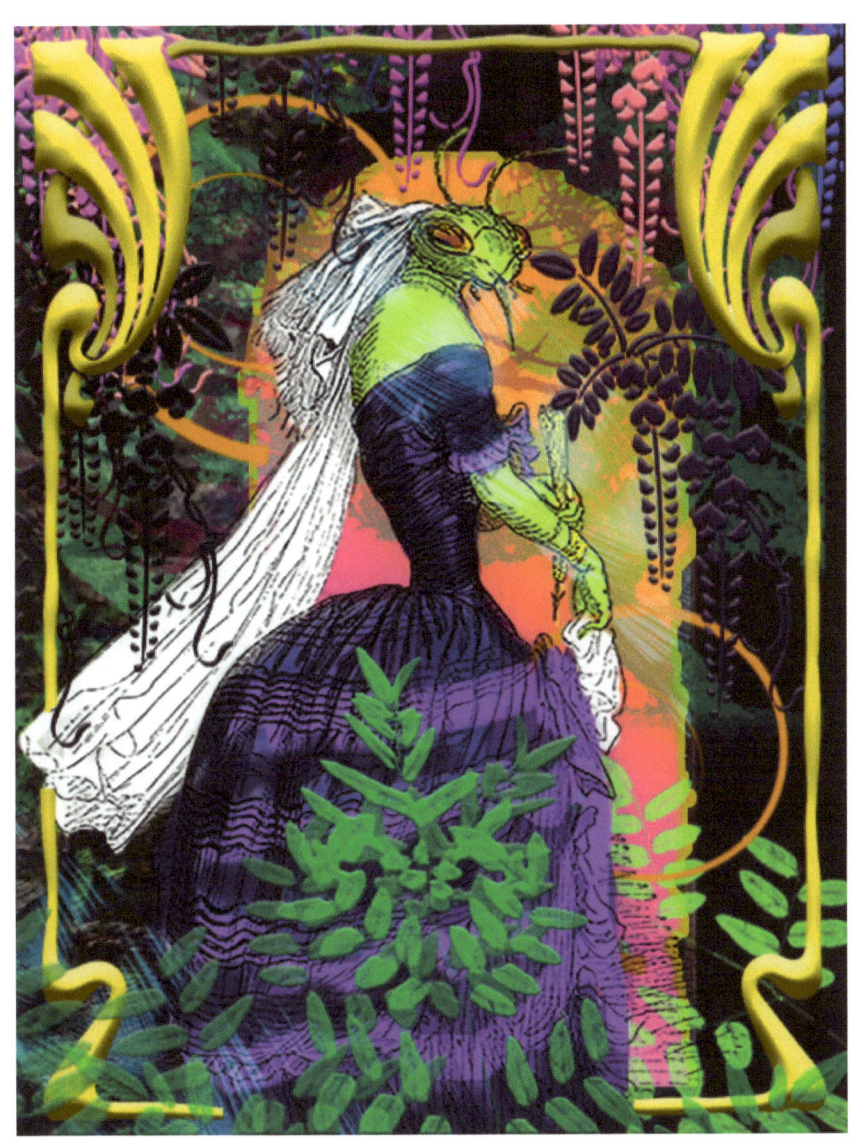

Gloriana

I waited in the garden, gathering strength, silent and splendid in the midnight....

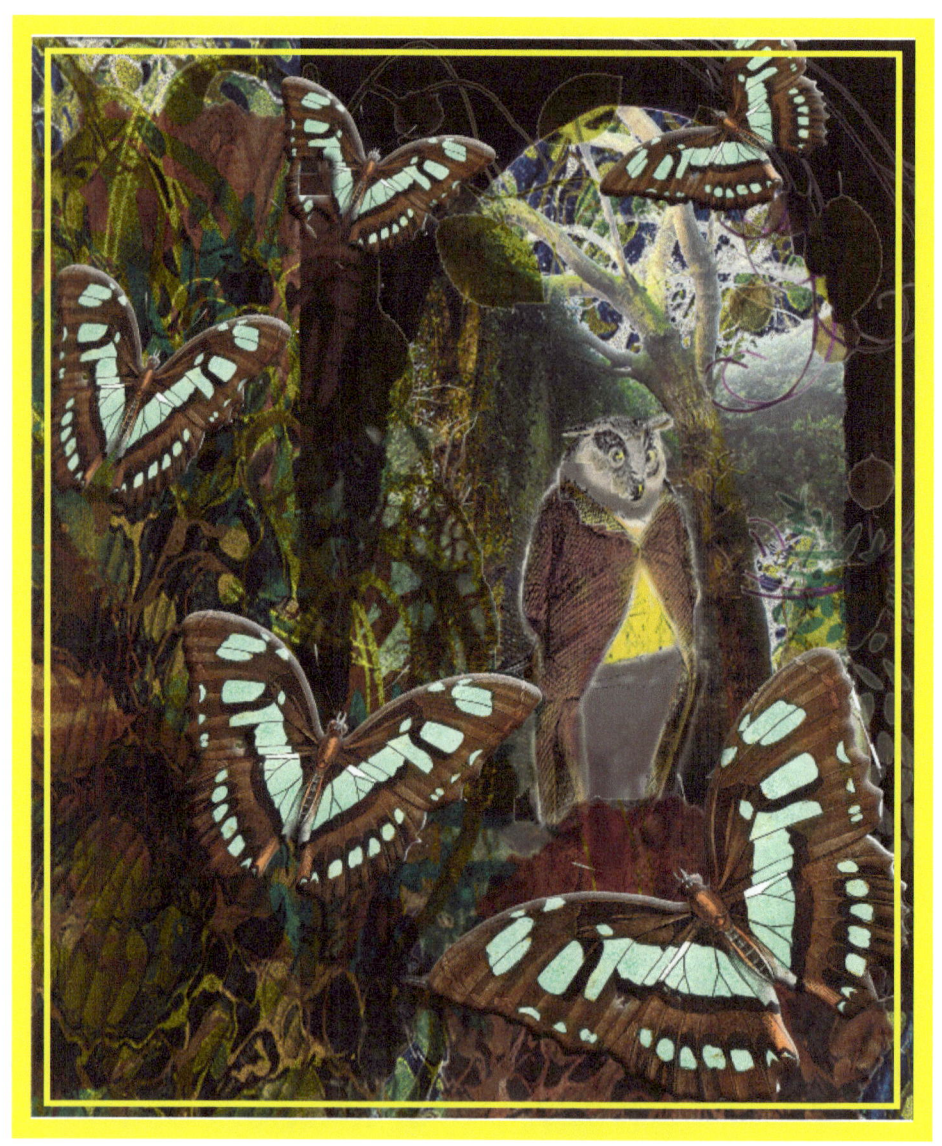

Old Mr. Owl

I married her when she was just a girl. She's still my girl.....

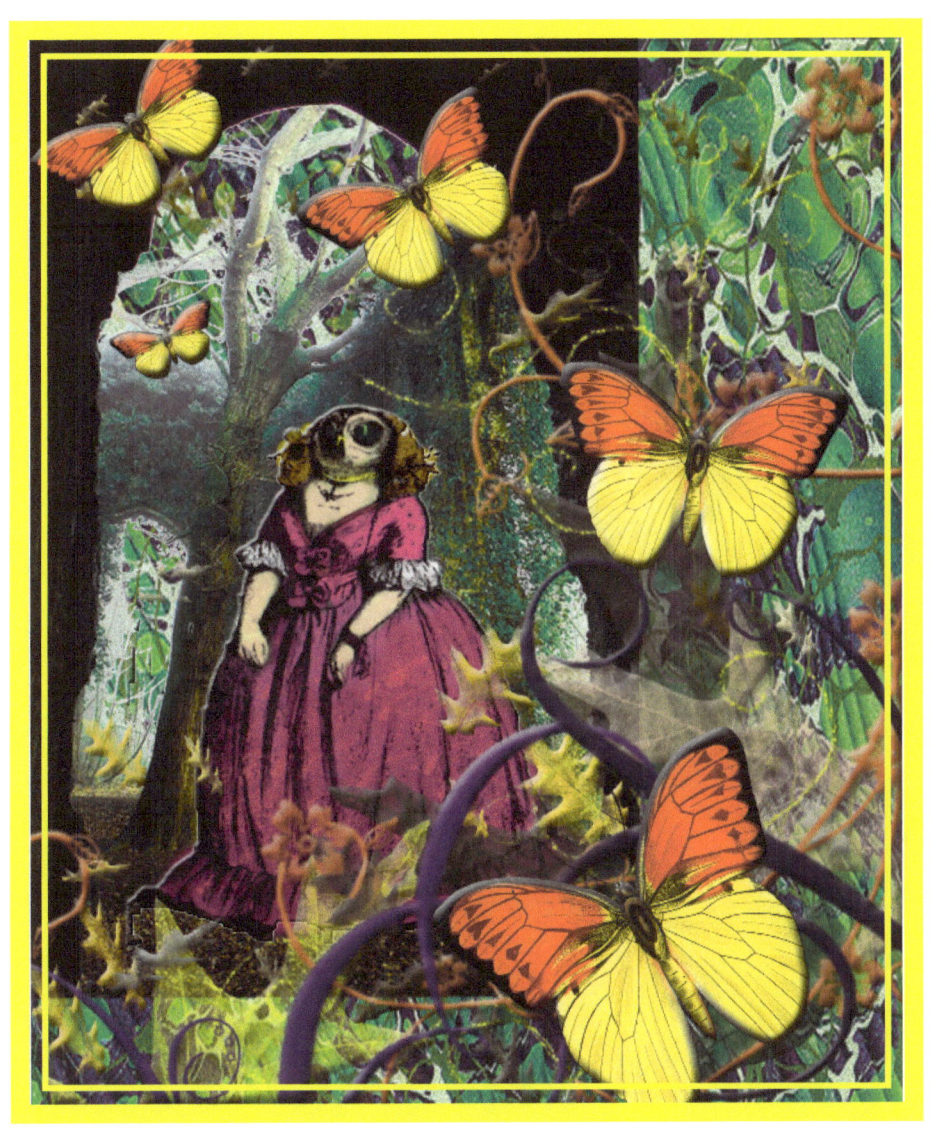

Old Mrs. Owl

He was always a bit less than handsome. But he was so kind.....

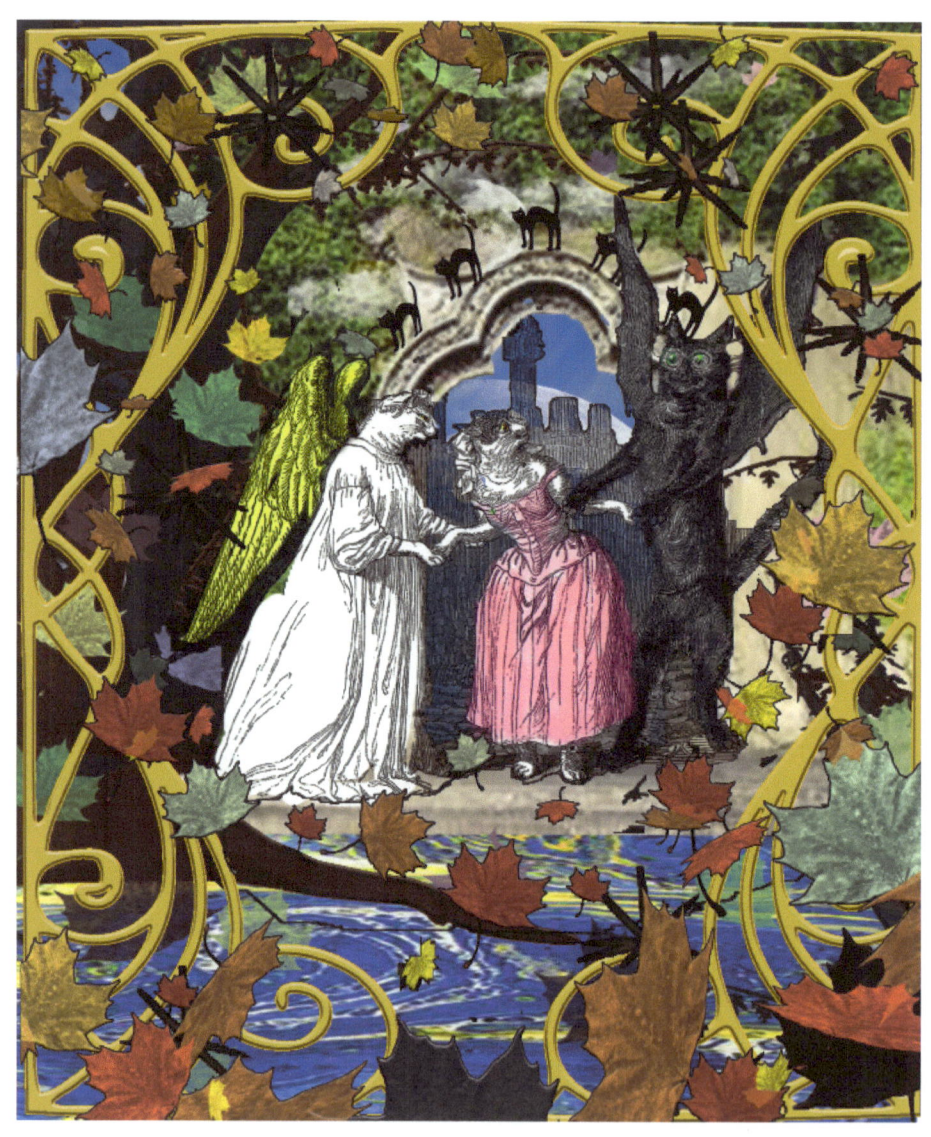

Tempted

Tempting but trouble either way....

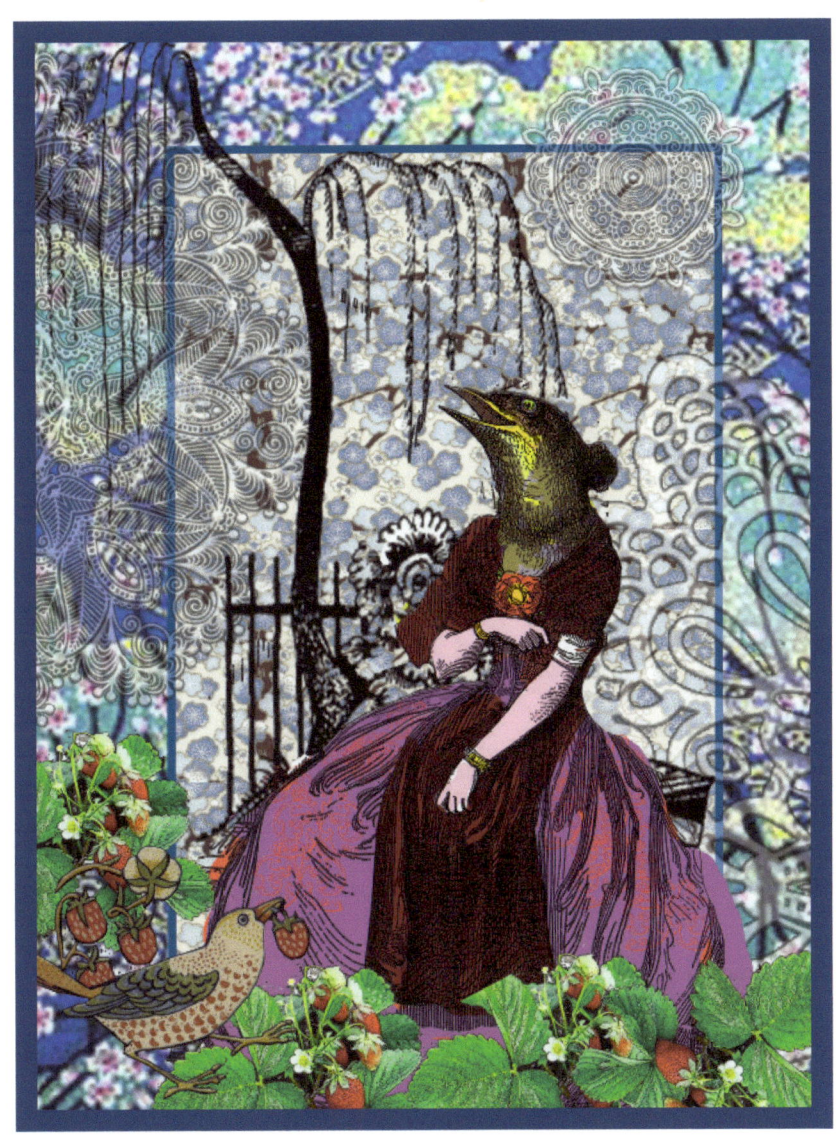

Sweet Gifts

Are those for me?

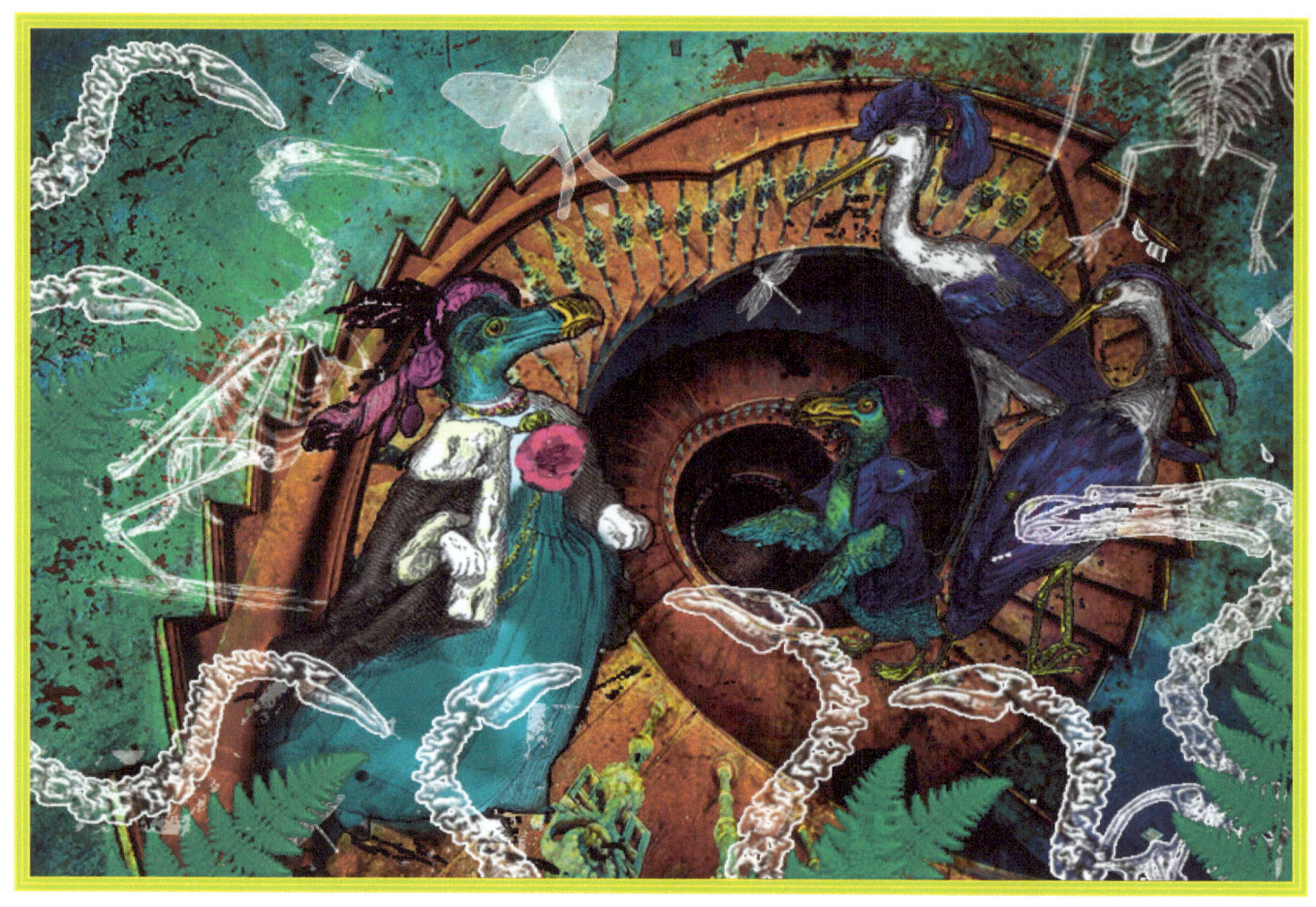

Family Resemblance

He's related to you through Uncle Freddie on your father's side...

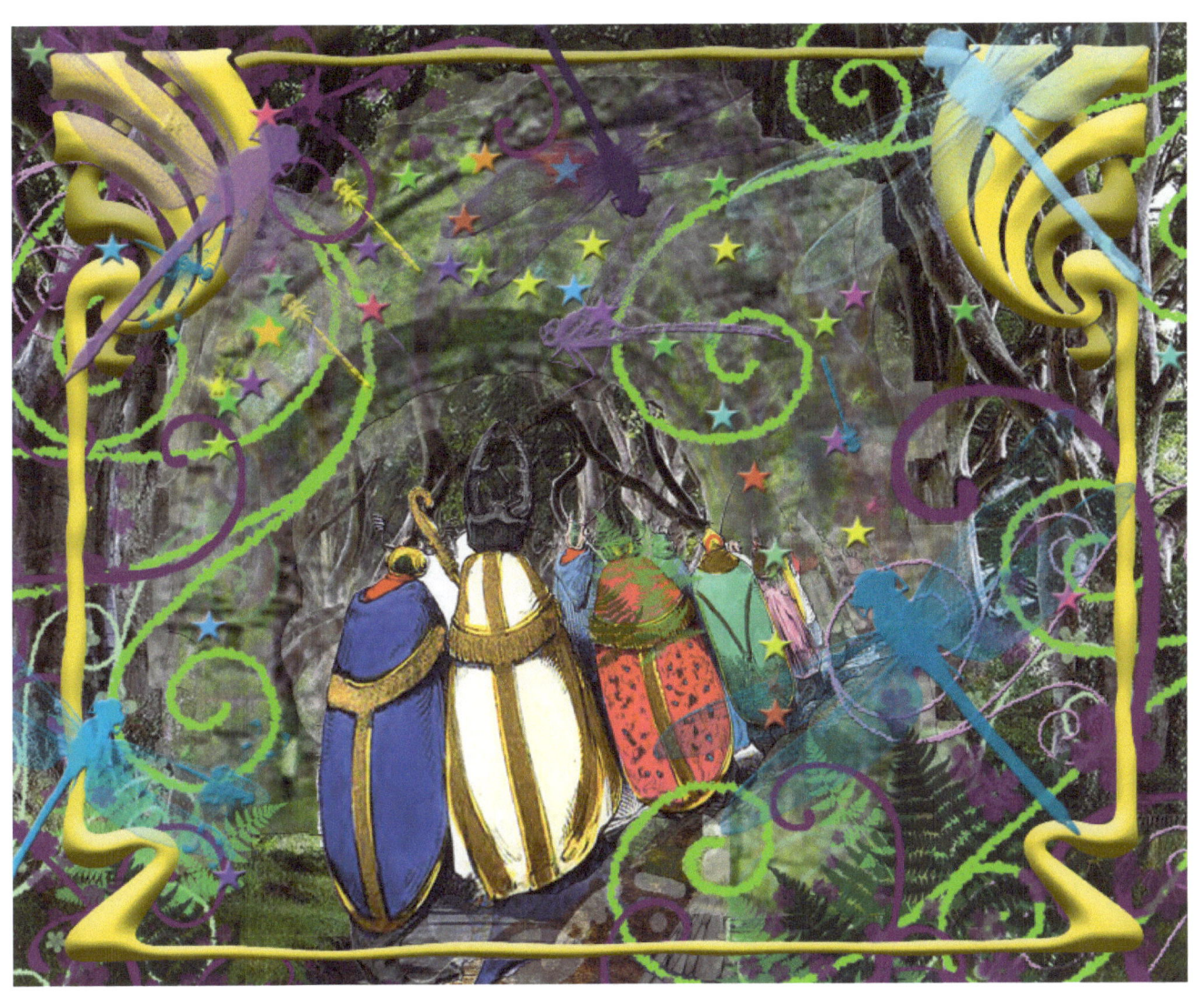

Processional

Holy, holy, holy....

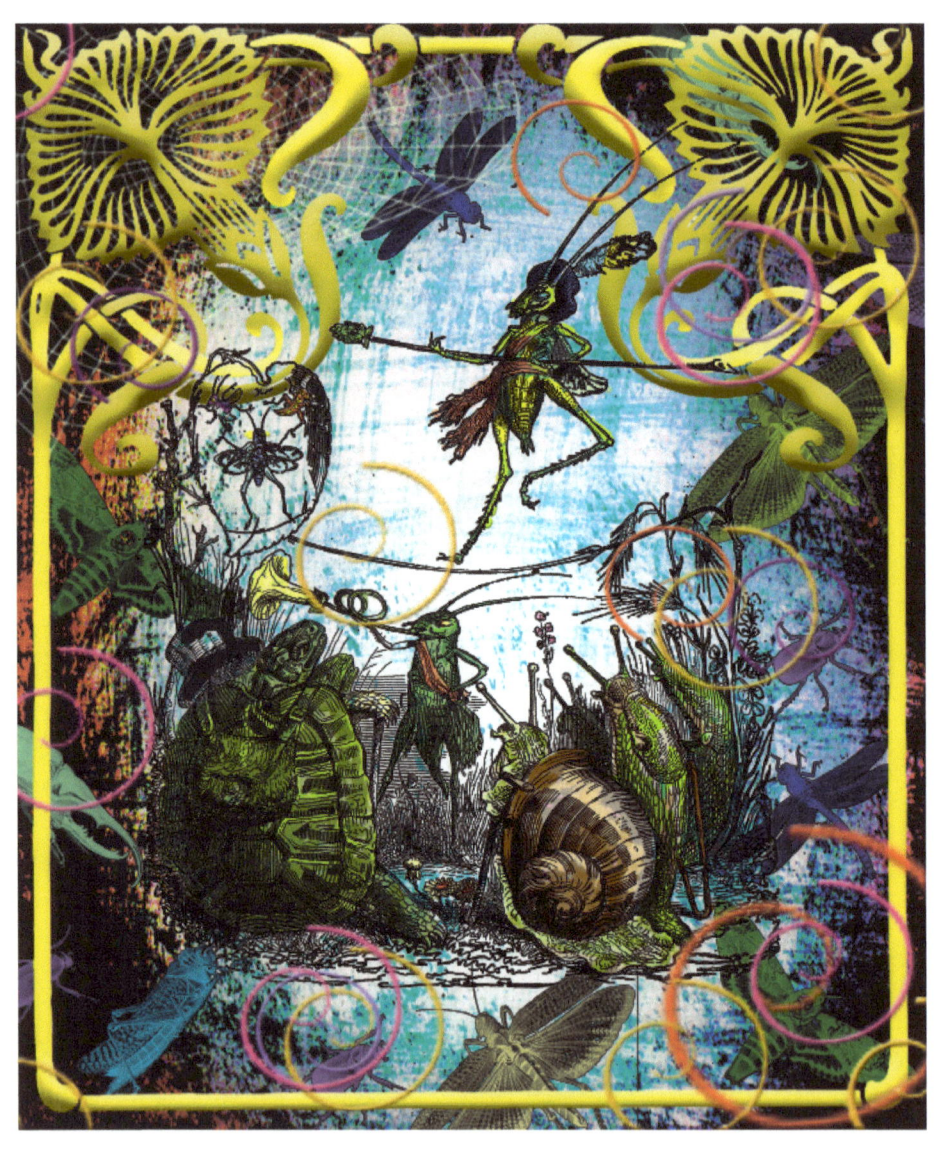

High Wired

A balancing act...

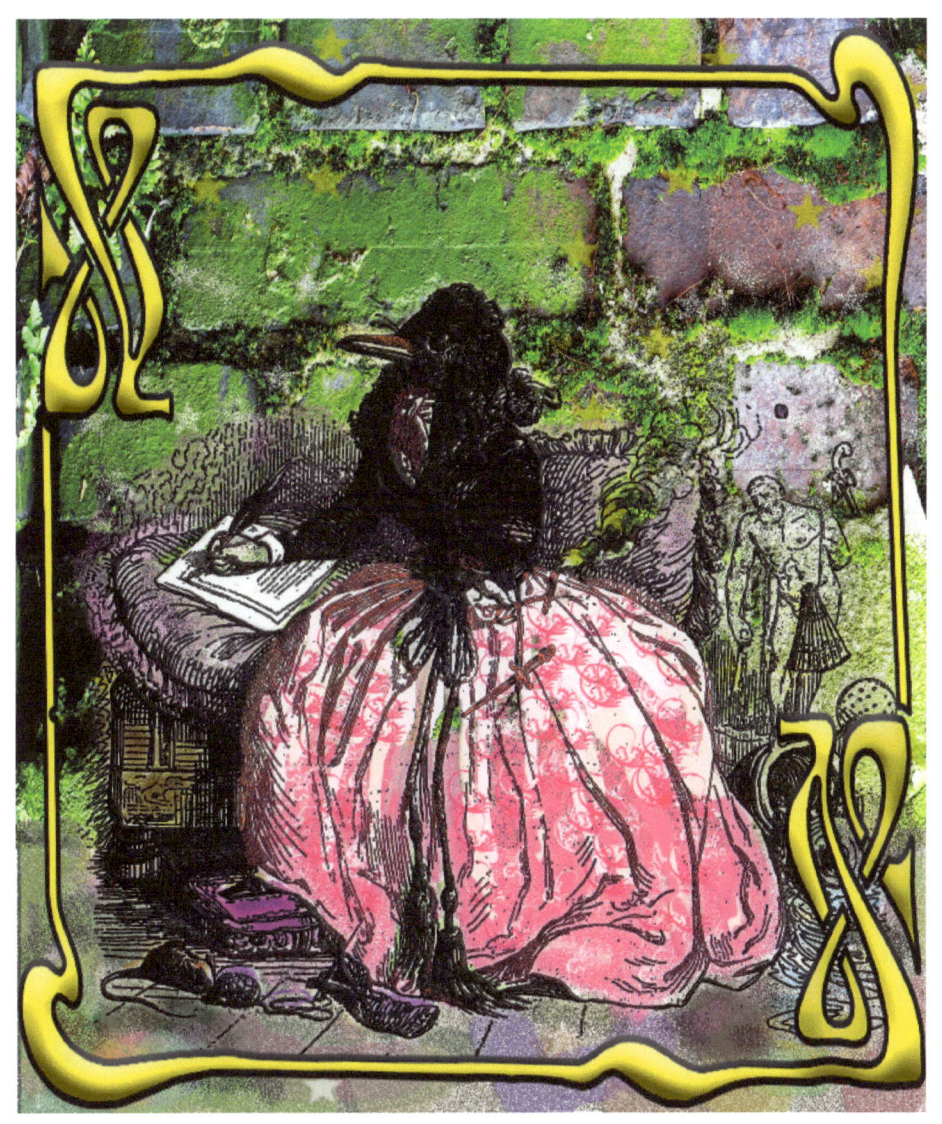

Missive

Dear John, it's with a heavy heart I take up my pen to write you....

Alice in Wonderland

Alice in Wonderland is the quintessential child lost. It's that tumble through a looking glass where everyone is mad. Either we join the dance or sulk on the sideline. But it's where we are.

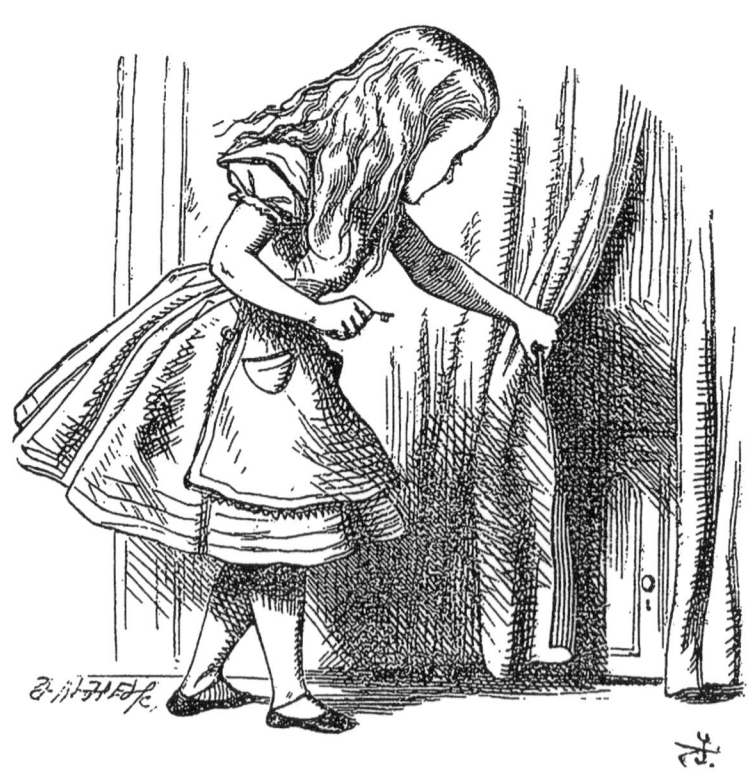

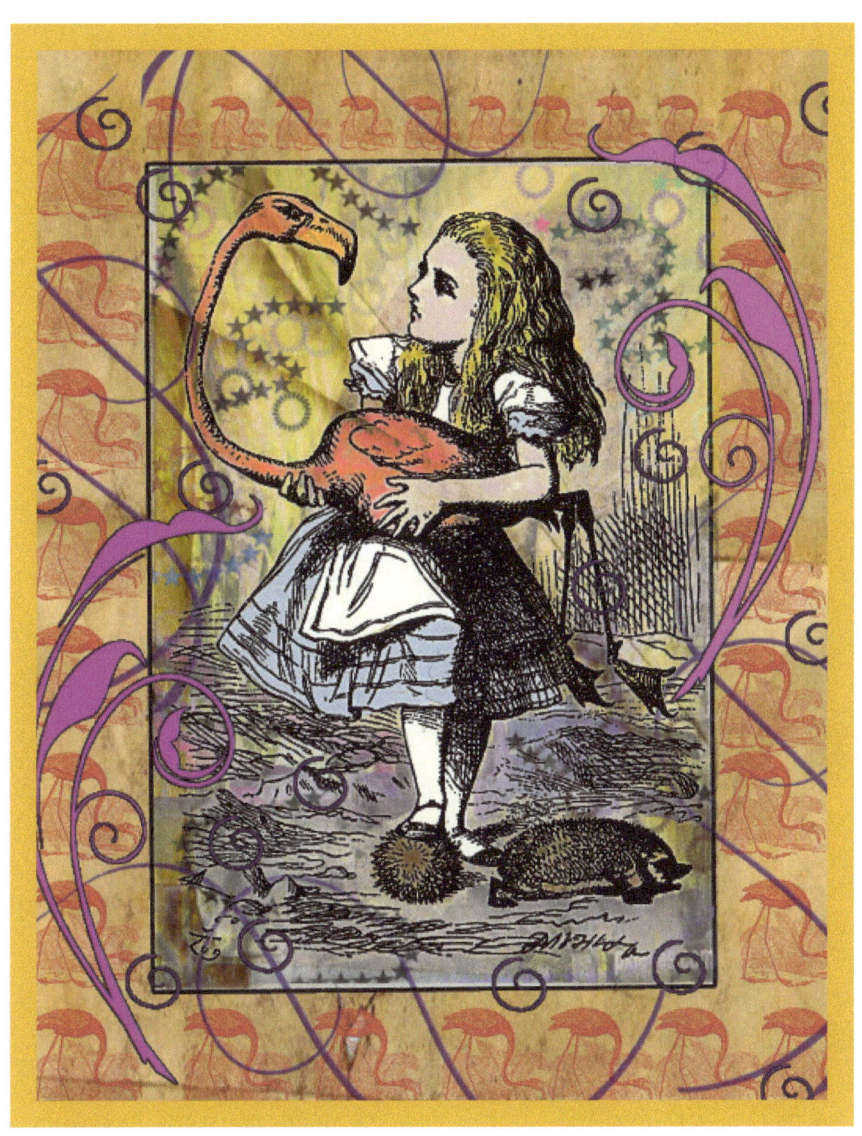

Flamingo Dancing

And that is when it reached out and grabbed my.....

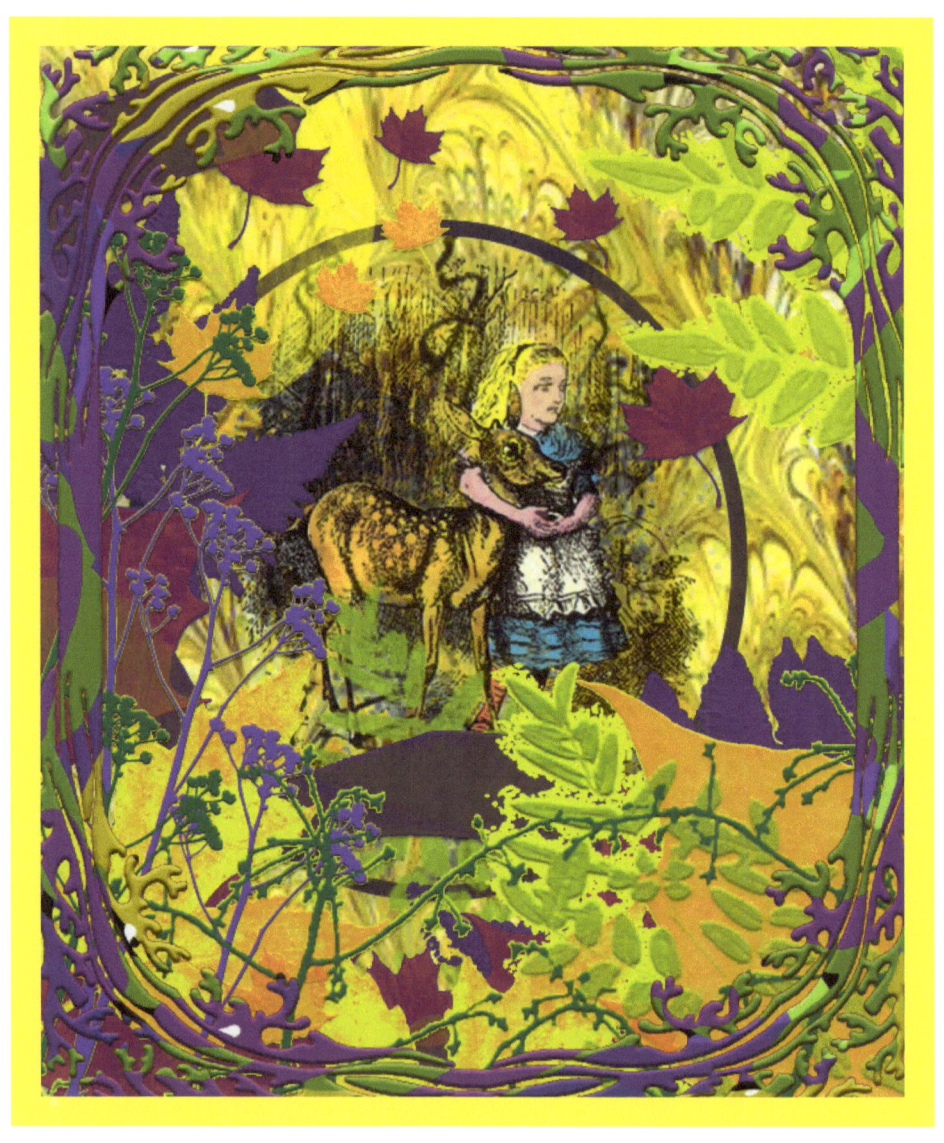

Fauna

Lost in Flora

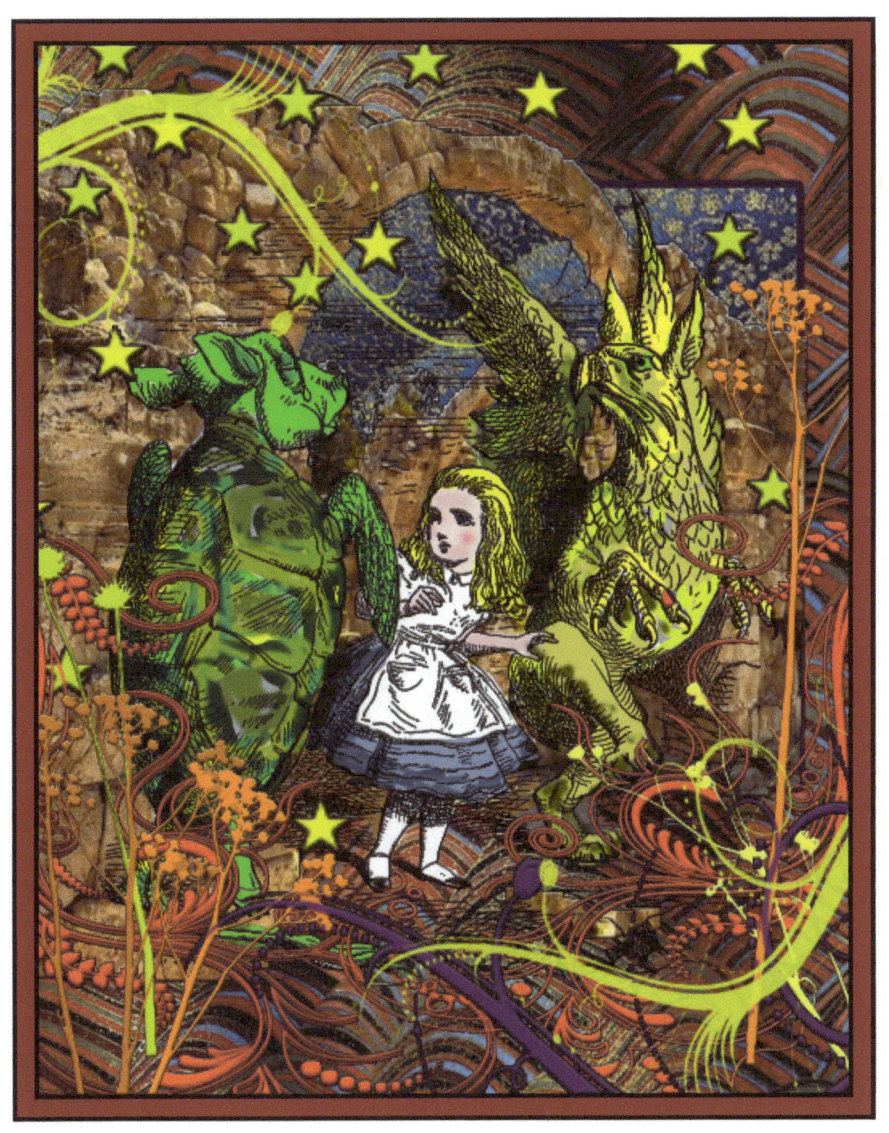

Texas Two Step

Line Dancing?

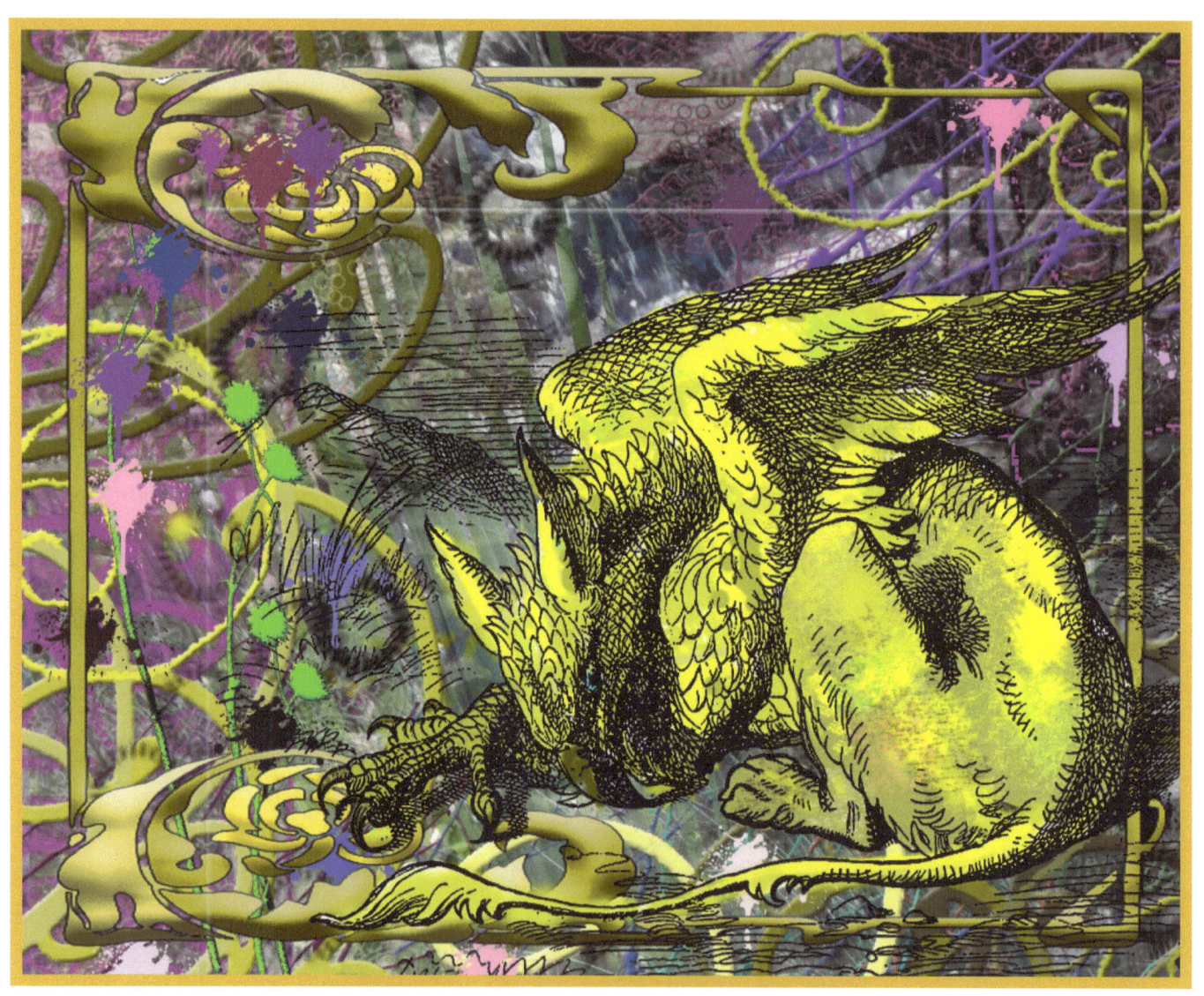

The Happy Nap

You could wake her but I'm not sure I would....

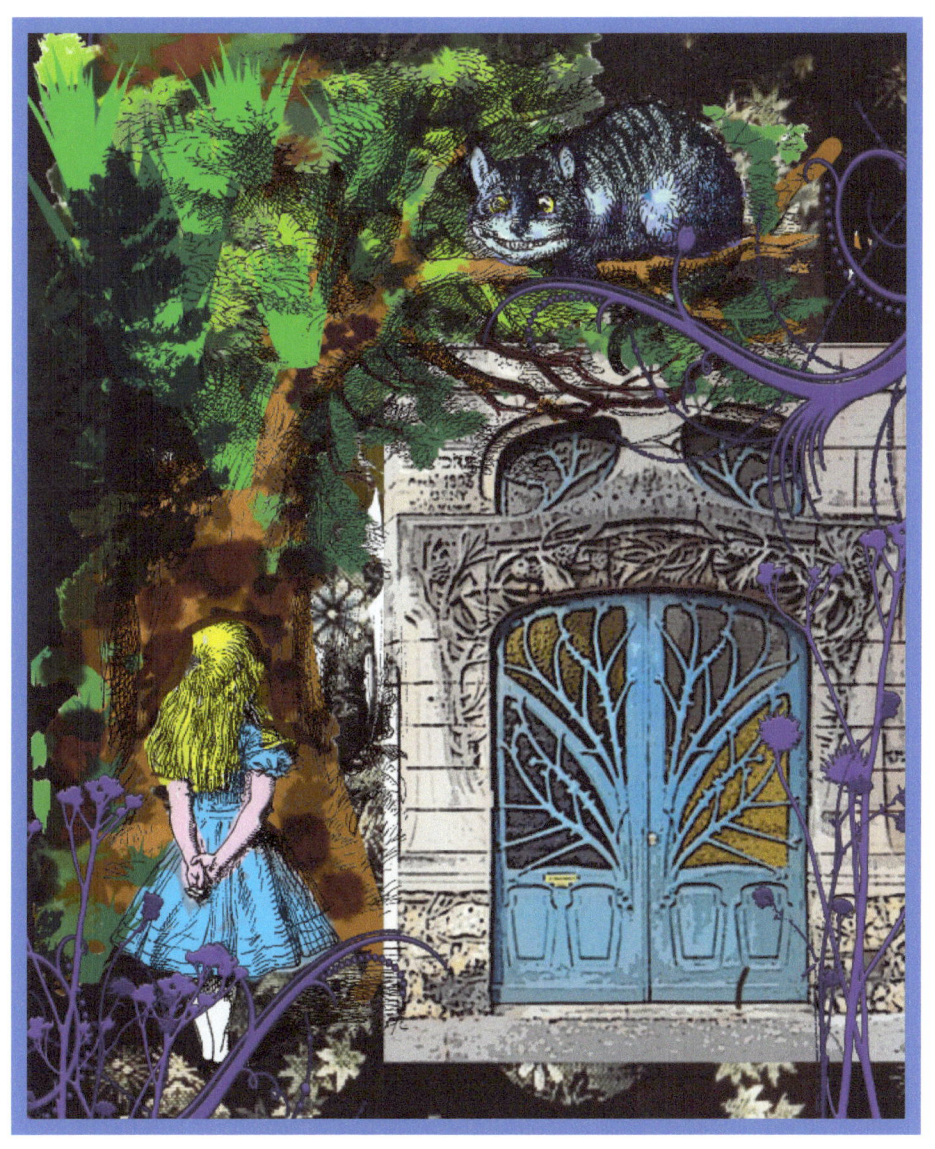

Choices

Well, you won't really know until you go through, will you?

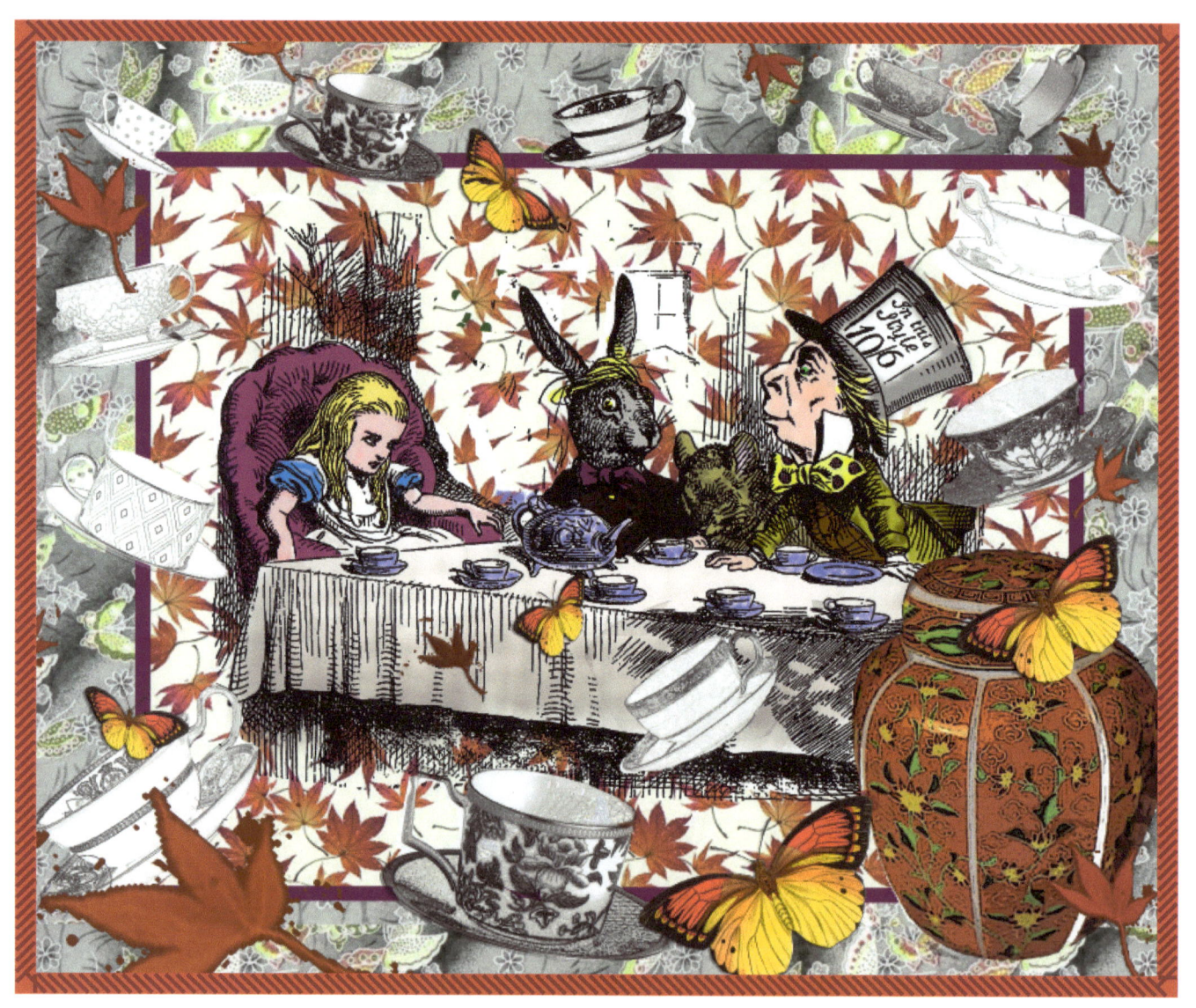

Tempest in a Tea Pot

I knew we should have kept the windows closed....

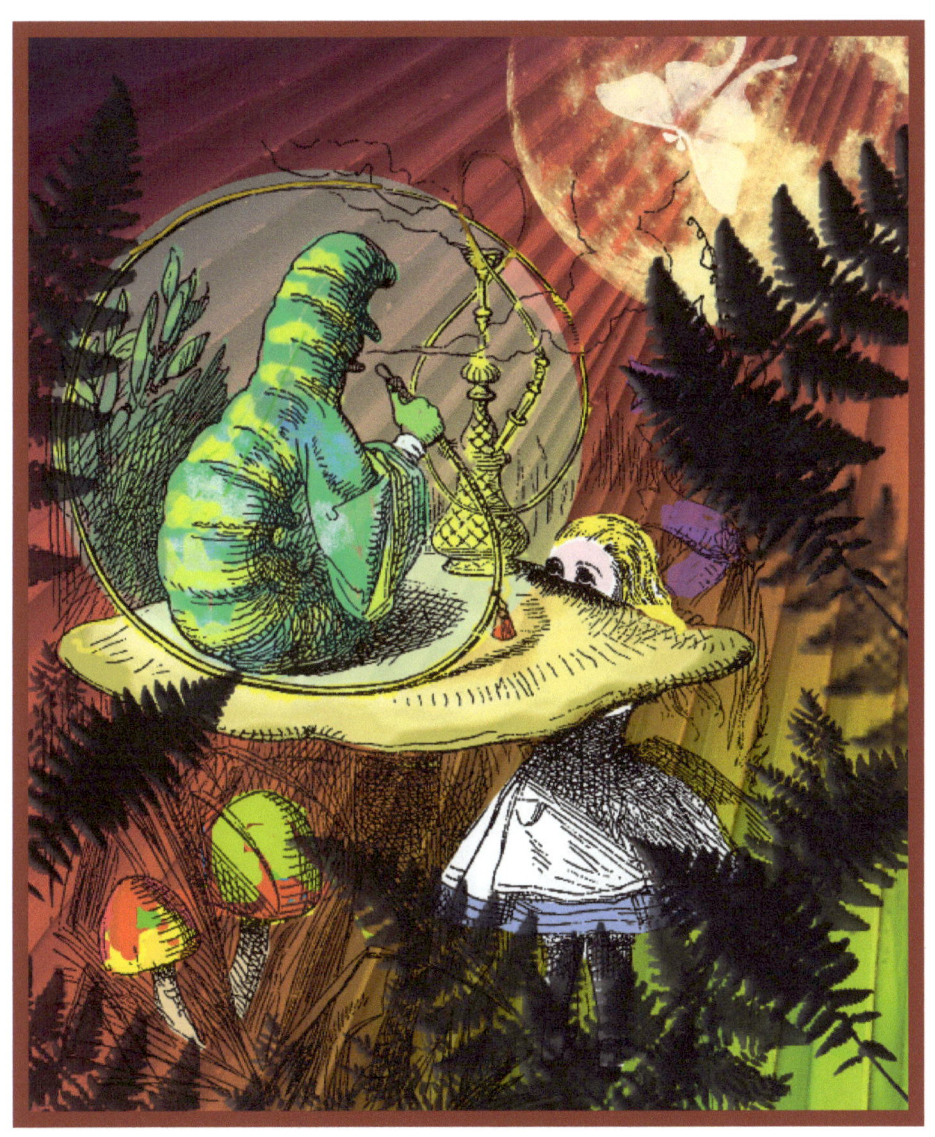

But Why?

Surely not all the answers can be because....

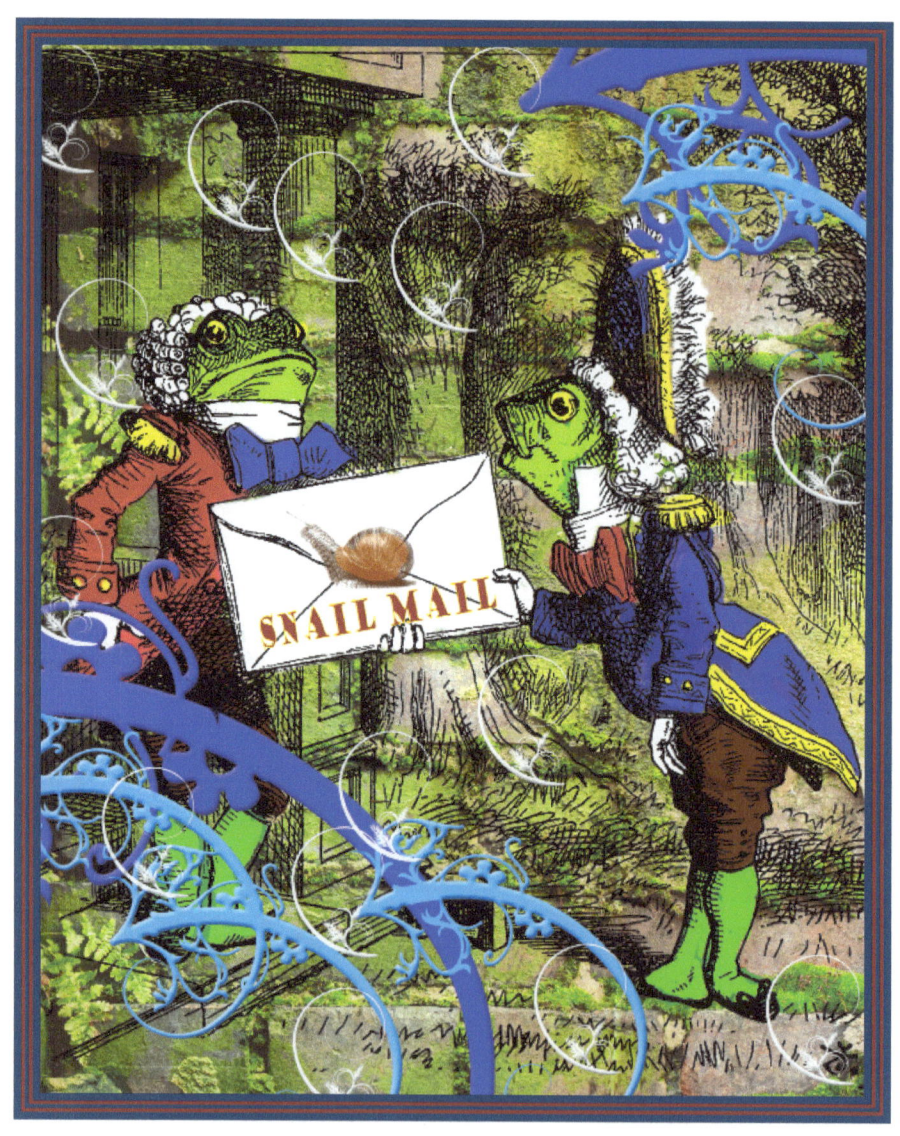

Snail Mail

I put it in the mail last Tuesday....

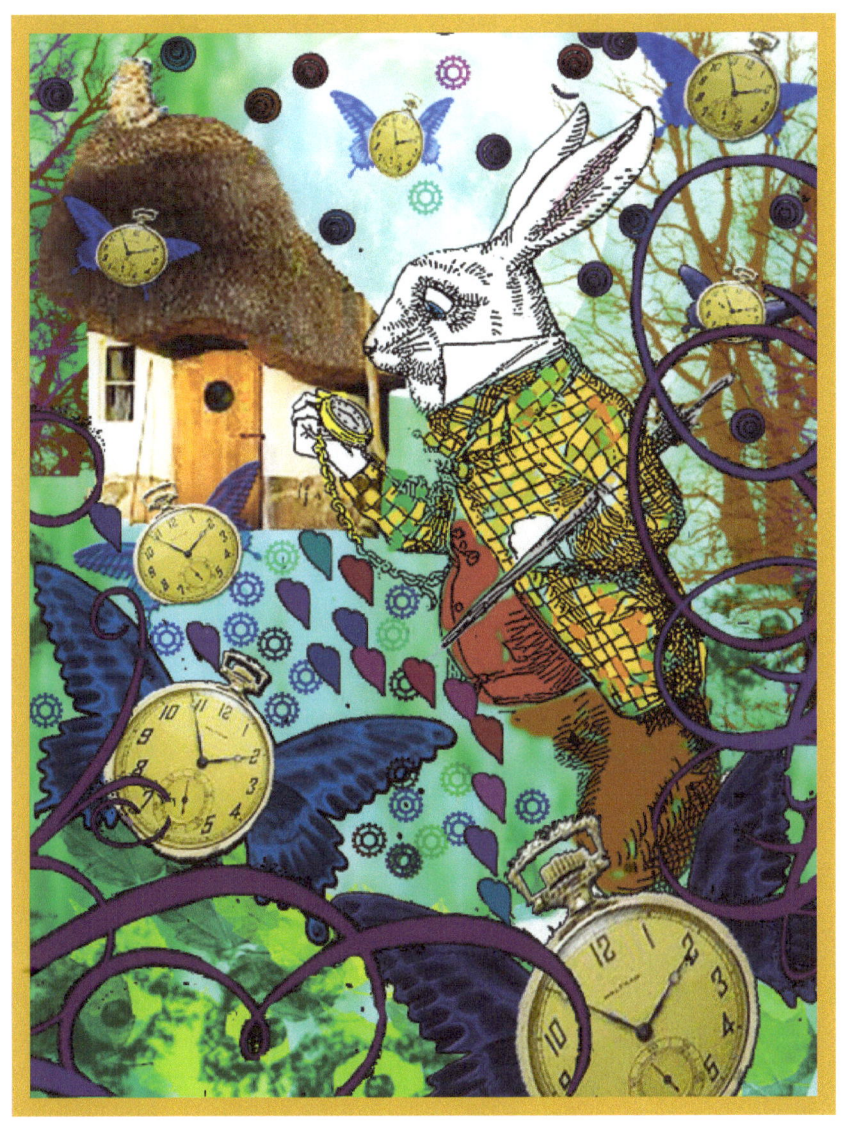

Knot Enough Thyme

Or rosemary. Or mint....

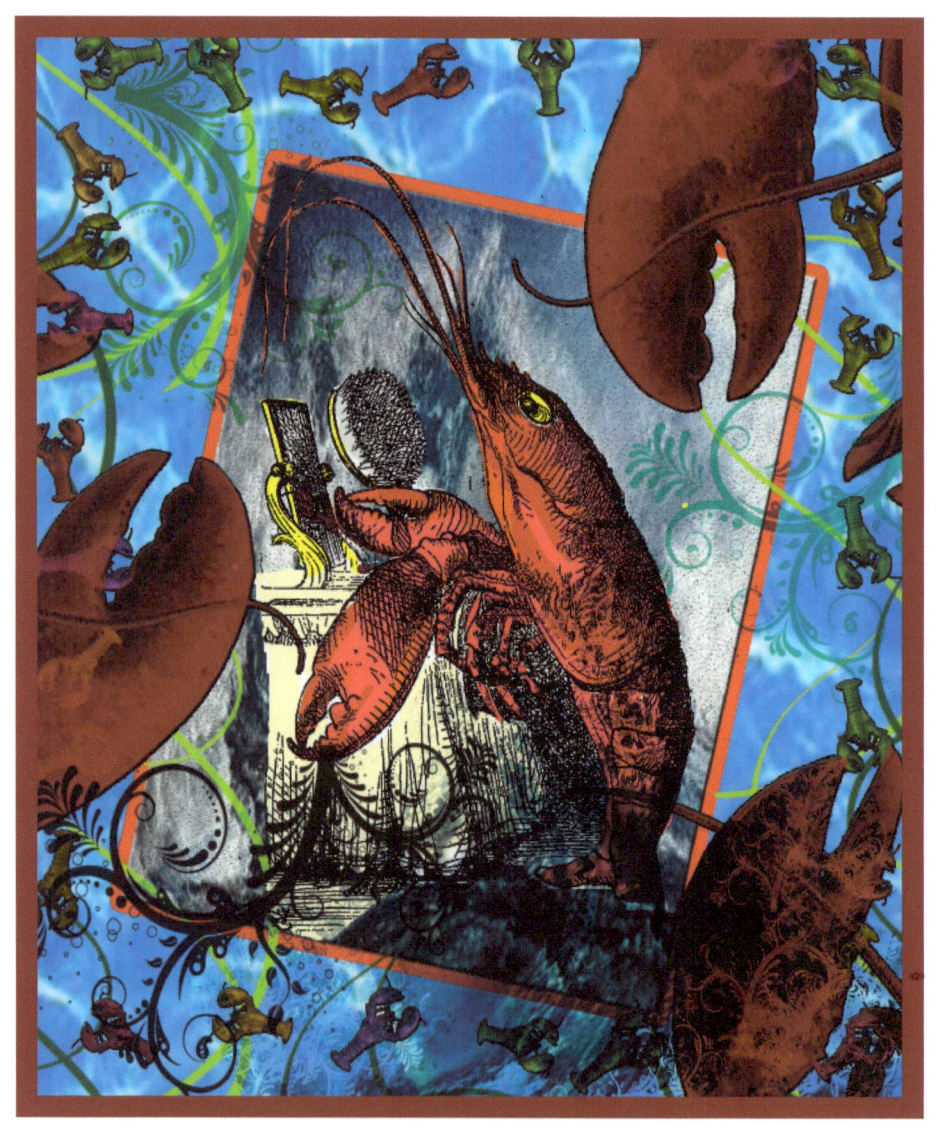

Stepping Out

A little texturizer on my tentacles, and a spit shine....

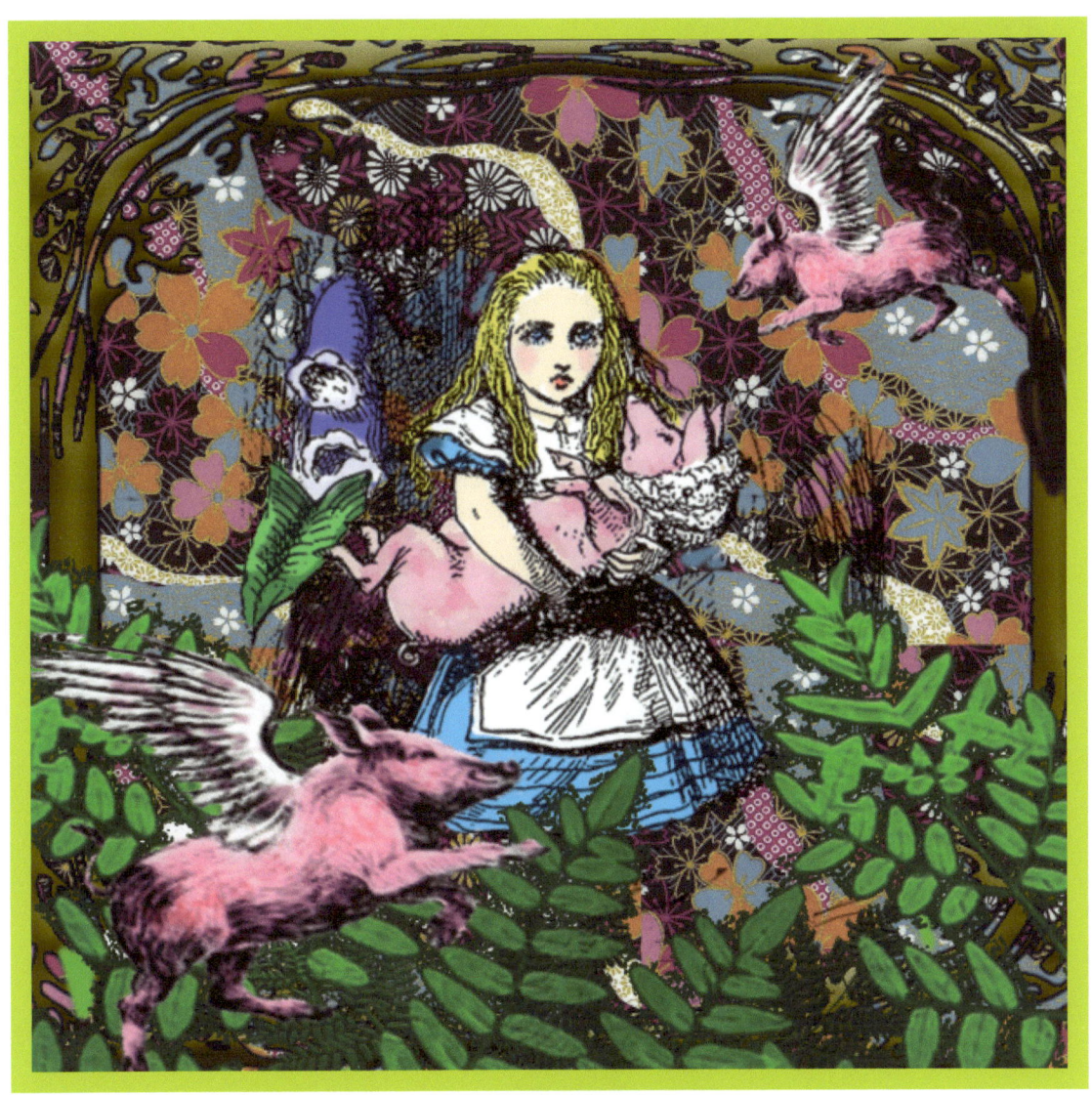

When Pigs Fly

And other disasters....

Dorothy in Oz

The Wizard of Oz books are another journey of the innocent through the unimaginable. The logic in Alice is by definition madness. The logic of Oz is magic. Both demand that we leave a part of ourselves behind and check our assumptions at the door. Here are some fabulous manipulated images from Oz.

Both R. J. Neill and W. W. Denslow illustrated various Oz books.

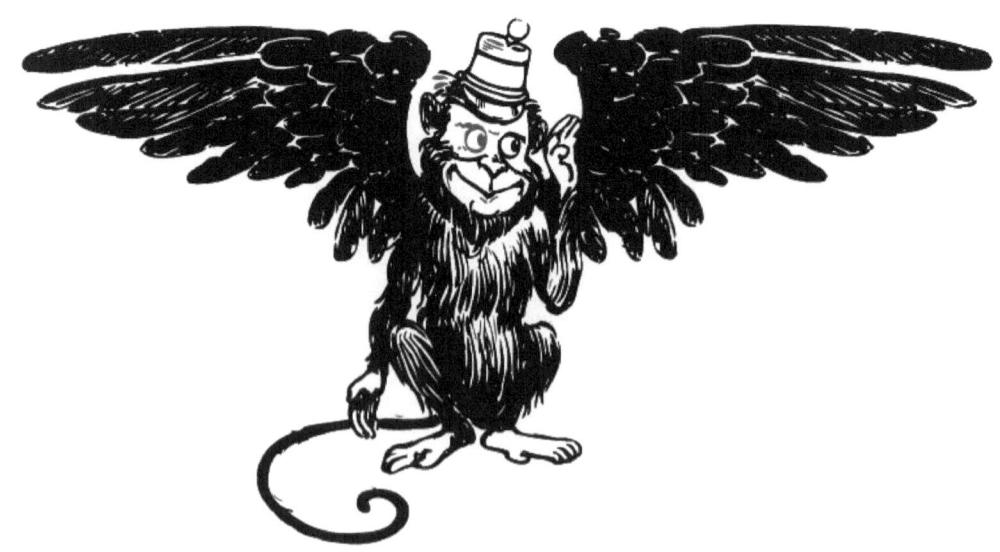

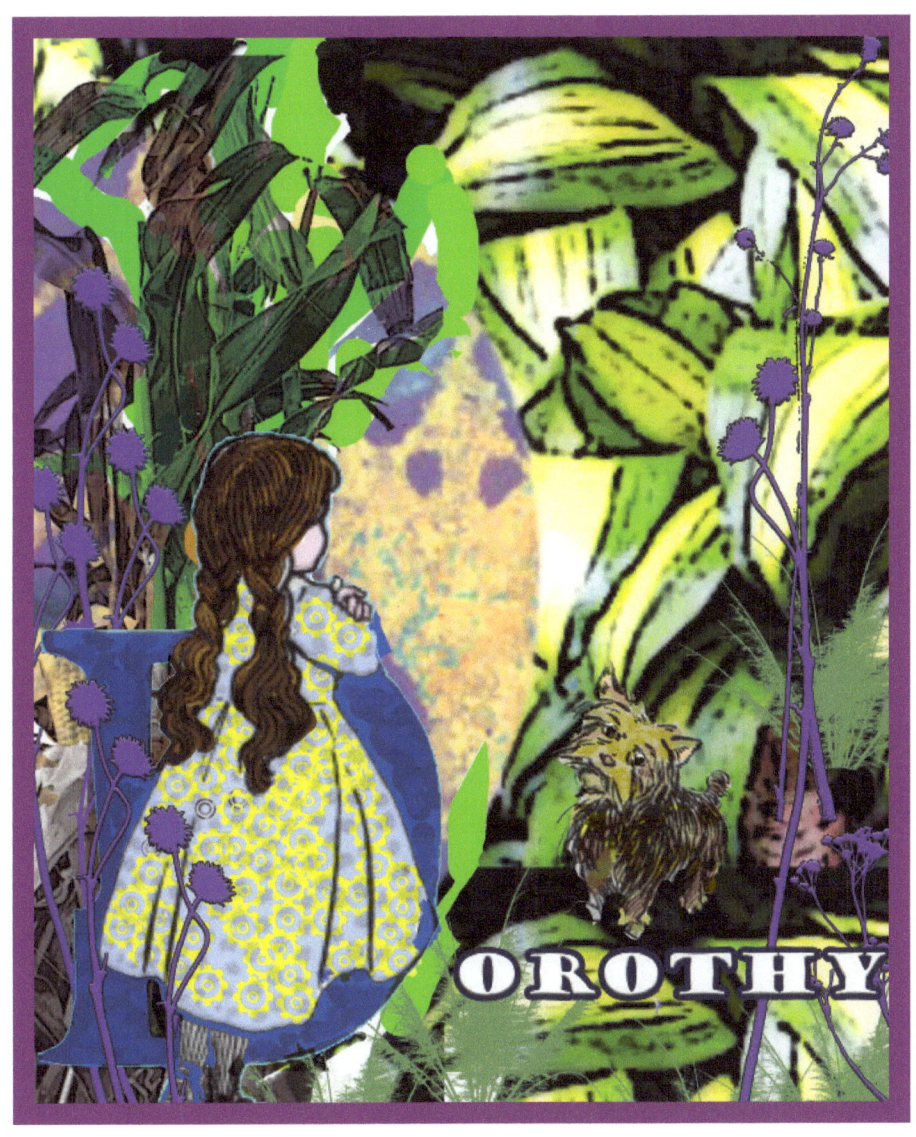

Dorothy in the Corn Field

No, it's not completely black and white...

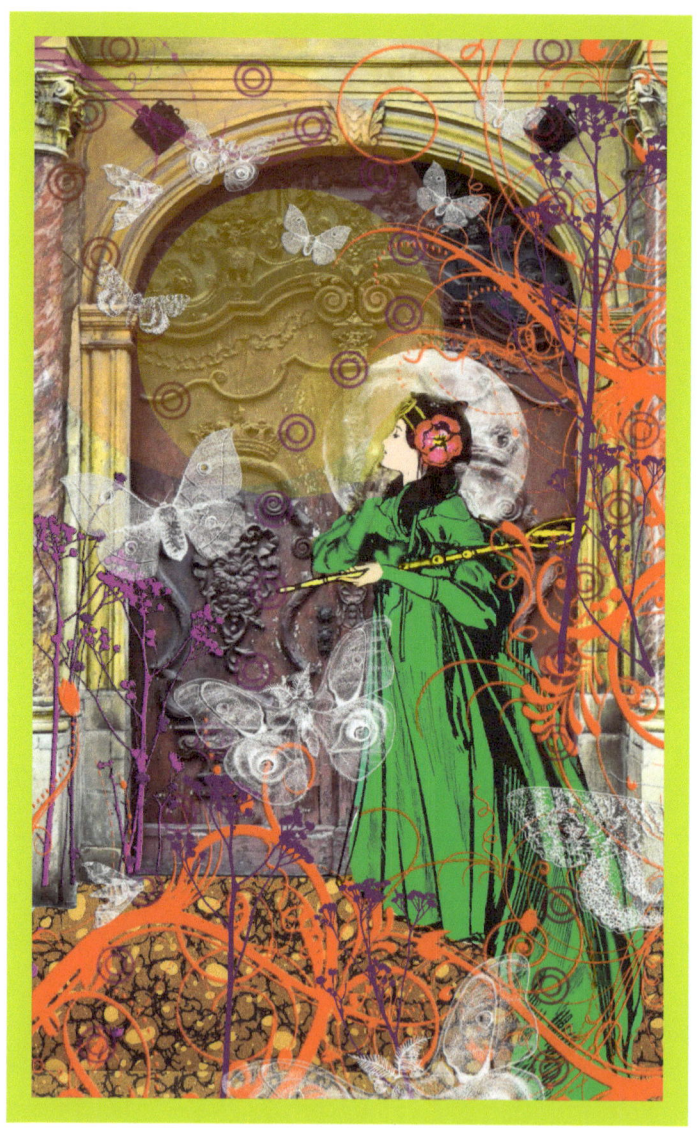

Walk up to the Door

Will it open?

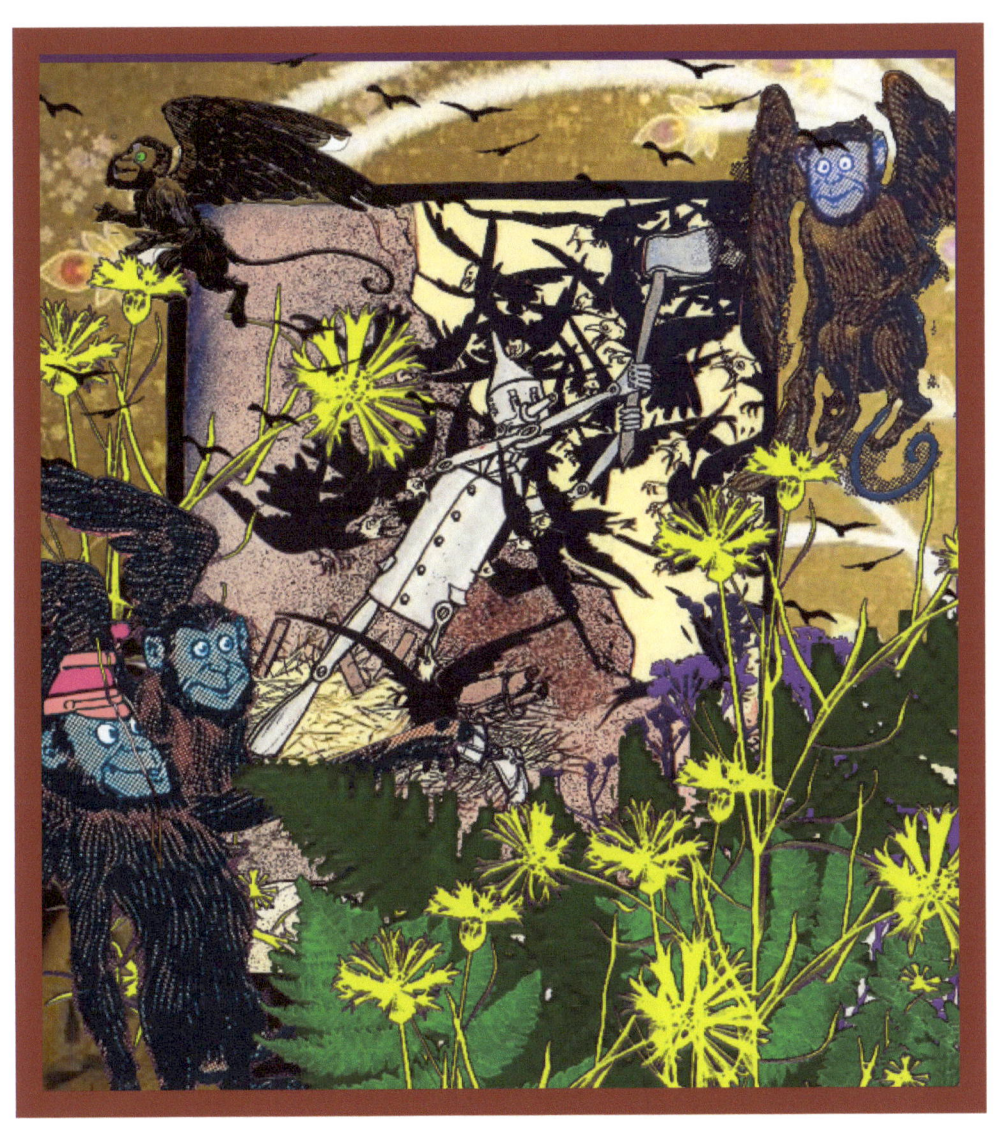

Not My Monkeys

Or my circus, or even my tent....

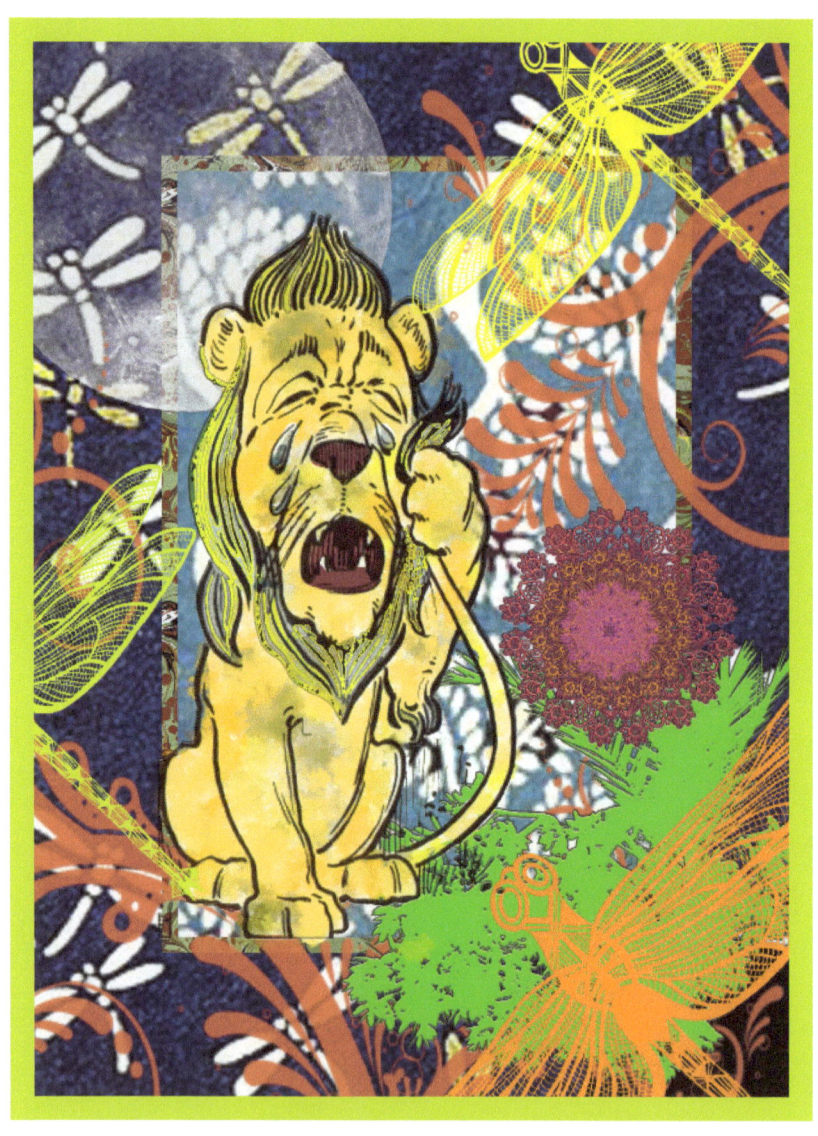

As Sad as That

Zinnias, and dragonflies and all....

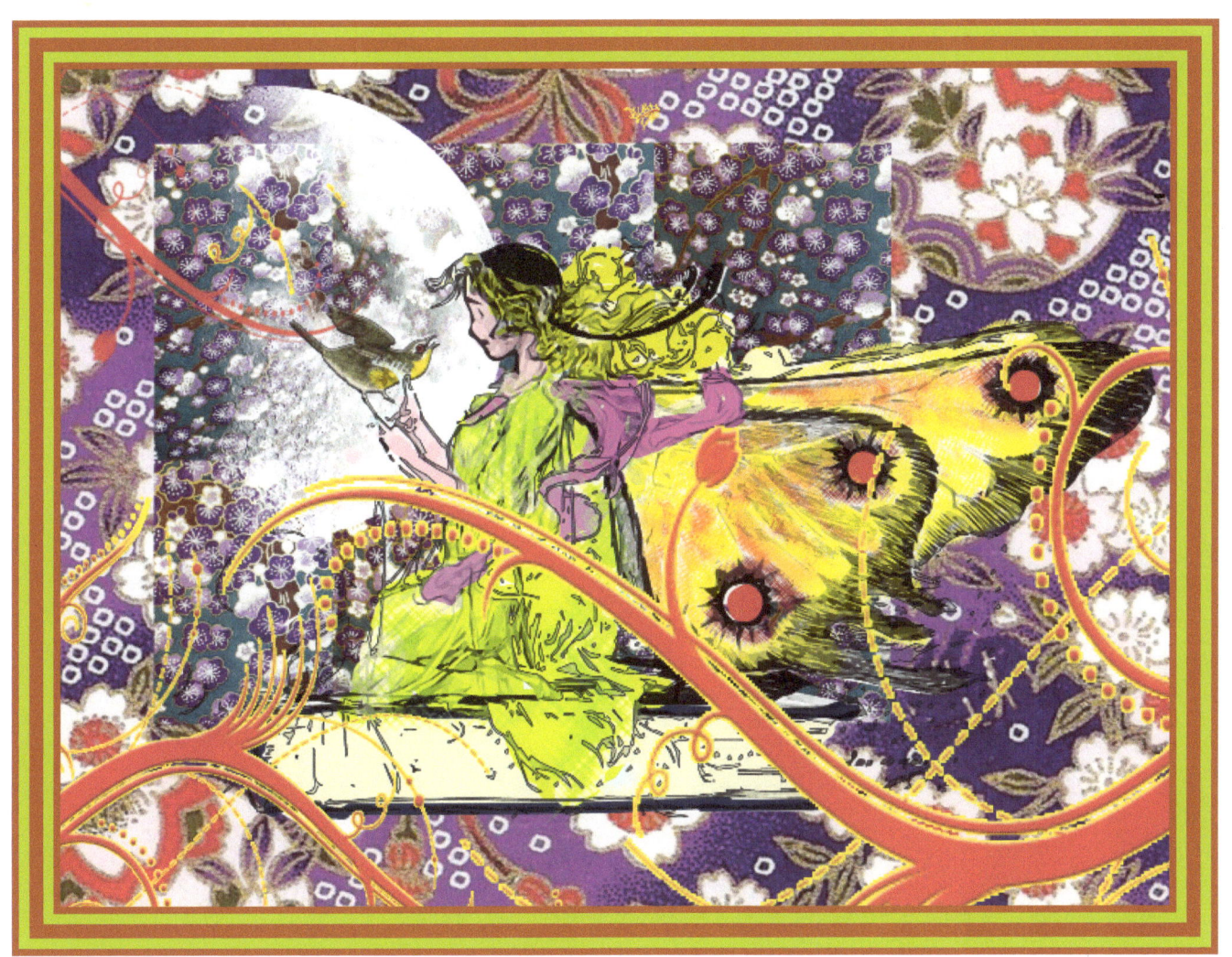

Whispers

The oriole always had the best gossip, so.....

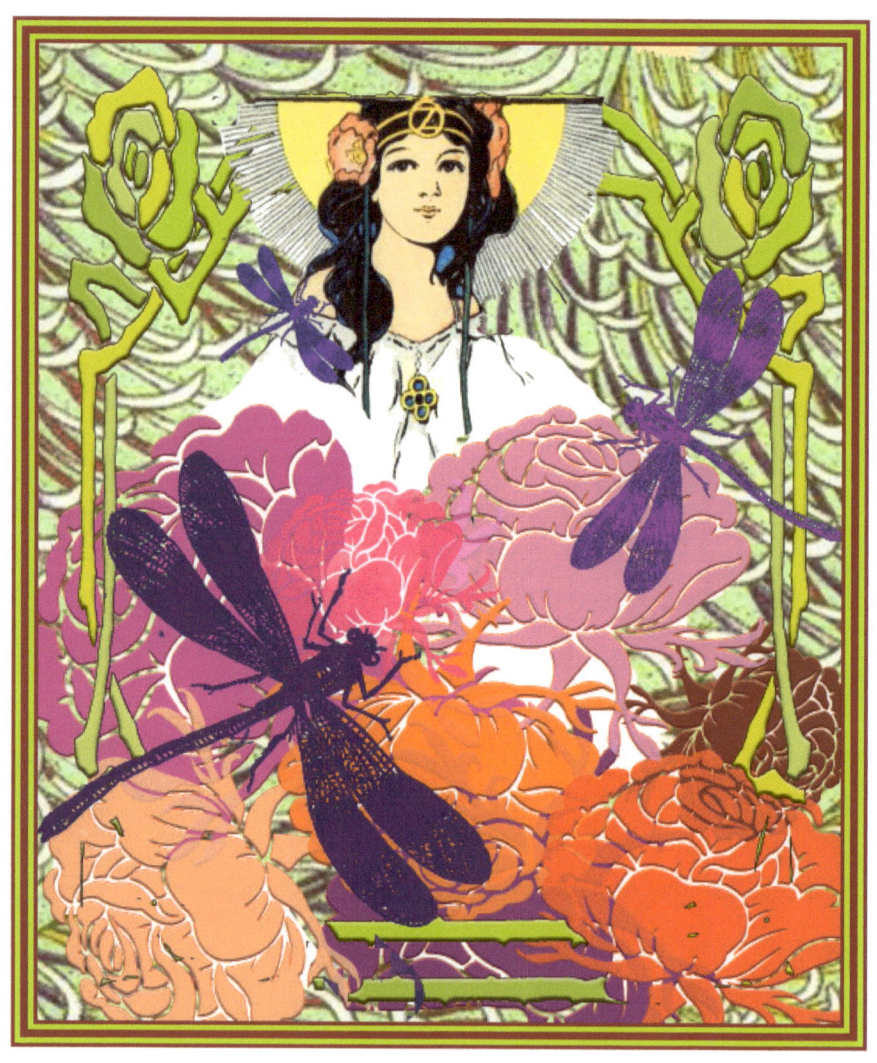

Garden Girl

Nestled with the dragonflies and roses...

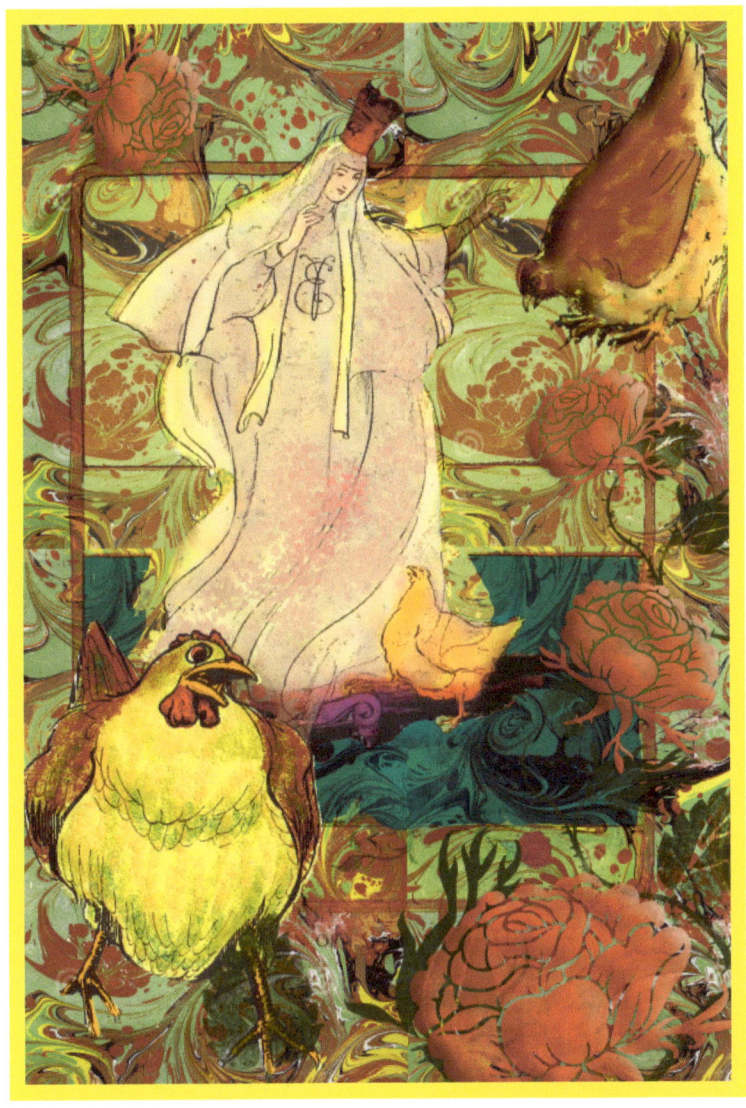

Feathered Celebration

We danced until the chickens came home to roost....

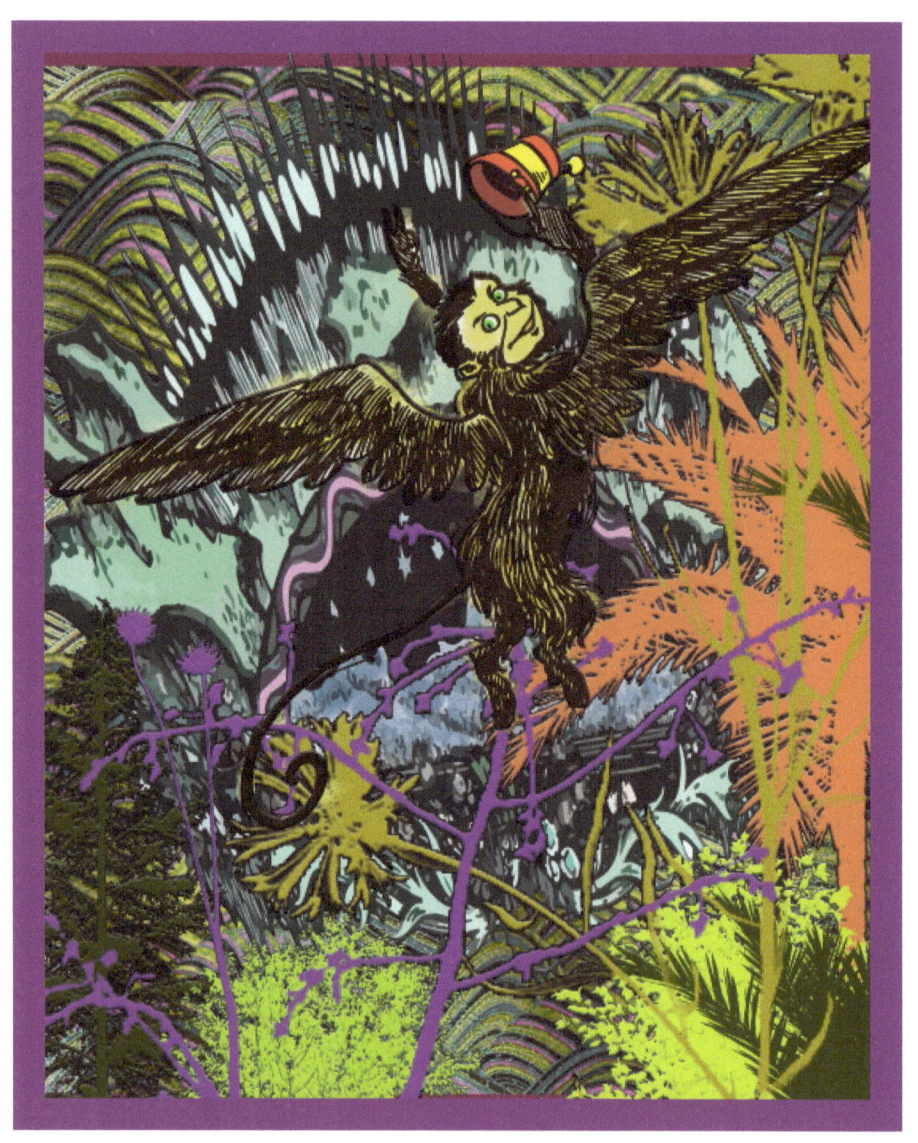

Flying Monkey Brigade

At your service....

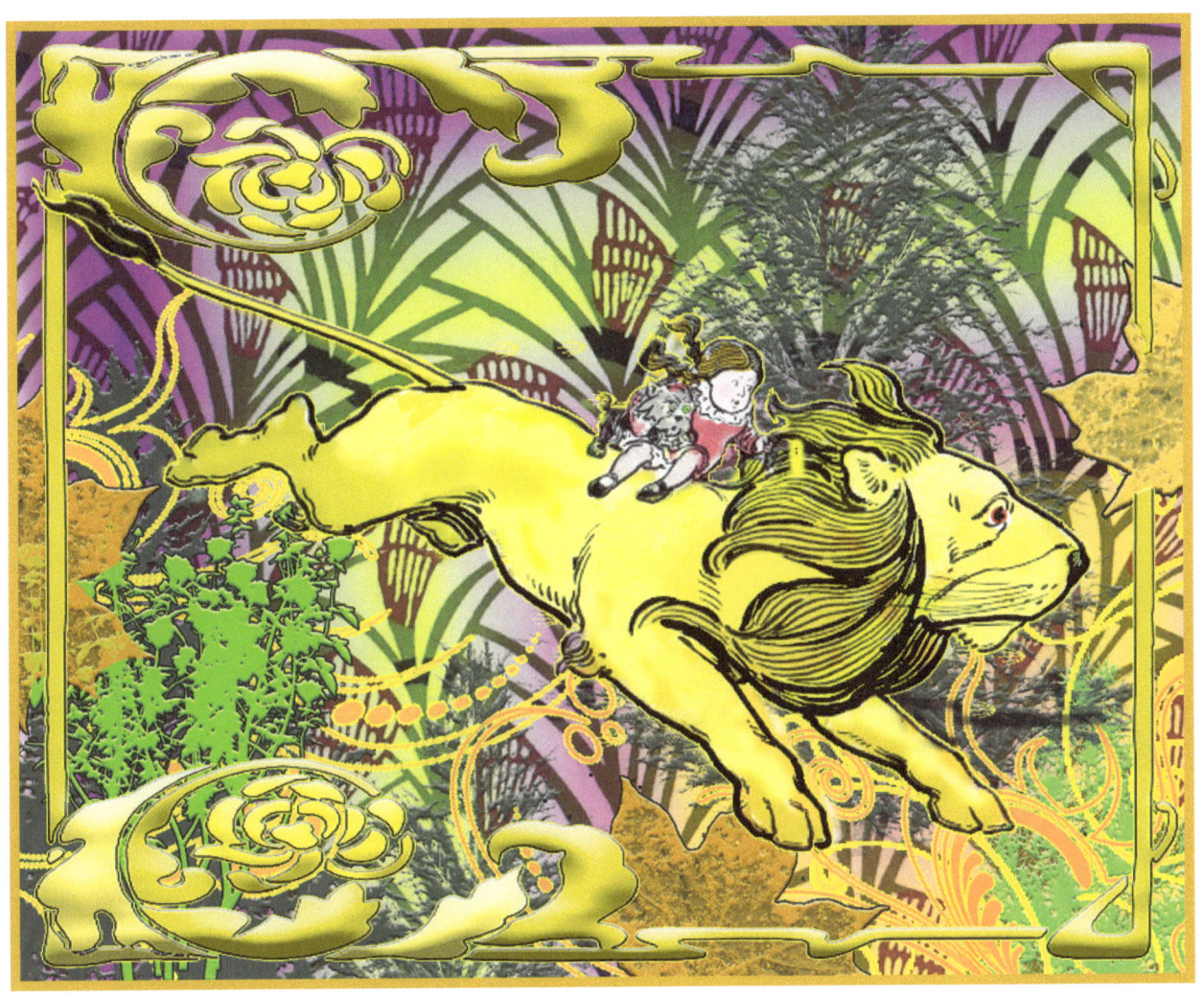

Traveling by Lion

Thinking is the best way to travel....

Flights of Fantasy Fly

What I love most about these illustrations is that they refuse to be confined to one story. They reach out to us to tell a million other stories if we are only listening. We are all the child in the wood, the cornfield, the unimaginable tea party. We are all looking for our place in the garden or the moonlight. We are always waiting for the stories to tell us who we are, what we need, where we are and what can be.

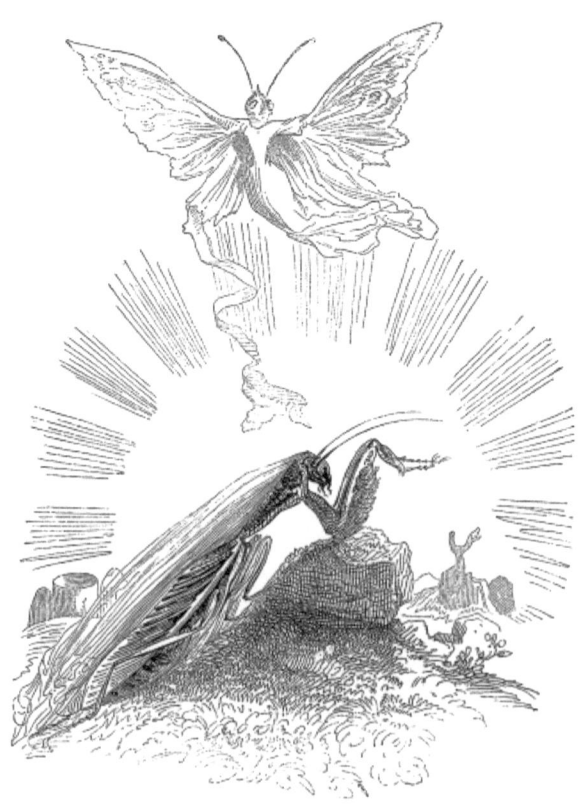

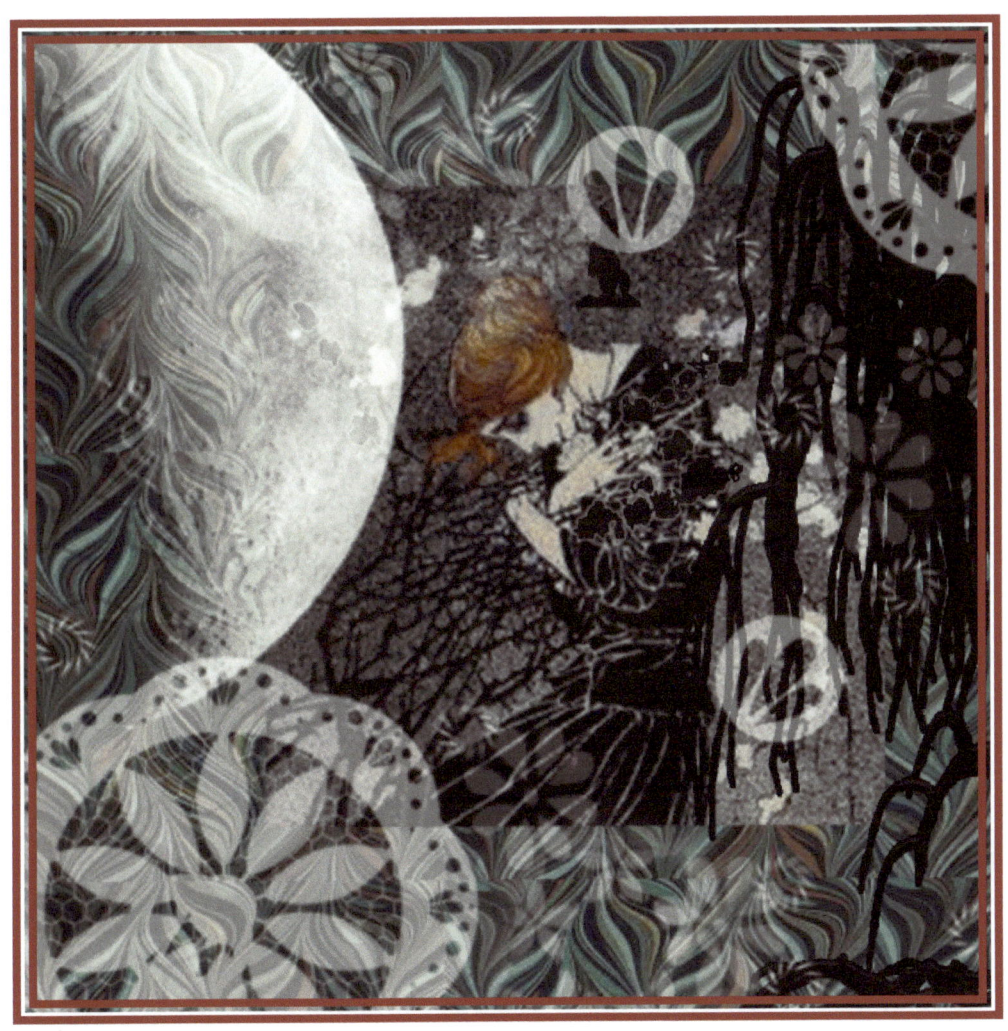

Spring Snow

Cherry blossoms in the moonlight....

Lady Fly

Step by Step
Layers on Layers

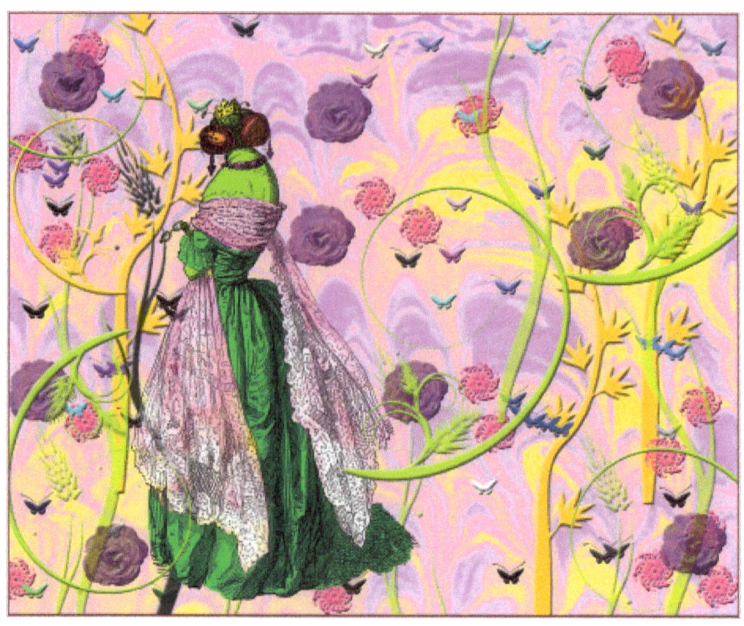

These images all began as a black and white illustration. They were placed into a colored background and set is a transparent level. Then I added a white background beneath the image and a third color layer between the two.

Finally I added other layers of brush strokes, that act like rubber stamps. These can all be outlined, embossed, made translucent or transparent. Finally if it needed a title that too could be added in.

As a final change, I could slide through different color groupings.

In one way it's very like the fiber art I've done all my life.

Except that I didn't have to rip anything out.

Background

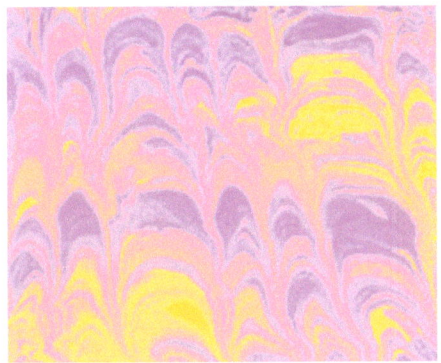

Marbleized Paper

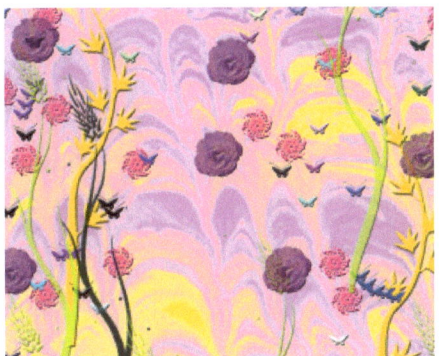

Brushes in Back

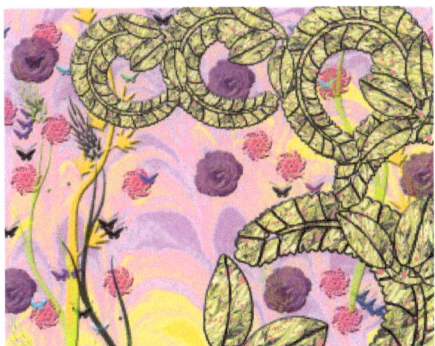

Brushes in Front

Image

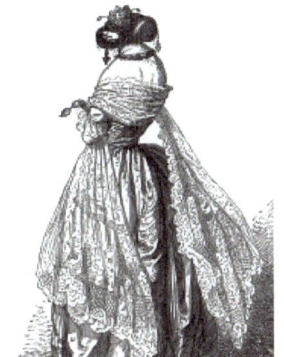

Original Image

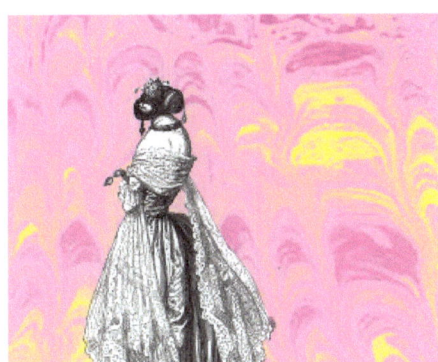

White Under Layer

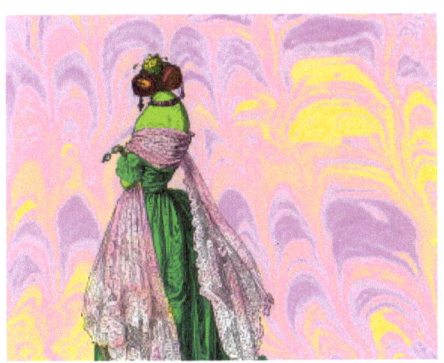

Color Layer

About the Artists

The original illustrations these were based on all came from books published in the 1800-1900s. Their illustrations have thrilled all of us ever since.

J. J. Grandville

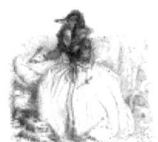

Jean Ignace Isidore Gérard, 1803-1847, generally known by the pseudonym of Jean-Jacques or J. J. Grandville, was a French caricaturist who Illustrated *Les Animaux.* See Conversations with Scissors, Cat Moon, Limelight, Old Mr Owl, Old Mrs Owl, Family Resemblance, Processional, High Wired, Missive, Lady Fly, Sweet Gifts, and Temptations.

Sir John Tenniel

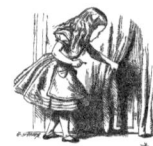

Tenniel, 1820-1914, drew the drawings for Lewis Carroll's *Alice's Adventures in Wonderland* and *Through the Looking-Glass and What Alice Found There.* See Flamingo Dancing, Fauna, Texas Two Step, Happy Nap, Choices, Tempest in a Tea Pot, But Why?, Knot Enough Thyme, Stepping Out, and When Pigs Fly.

W. W. Denslow

Denslow, 1856-1915, illustrated the original *Dorothy and the Wizard of Oz,* and some of the earlier books by Frank Baum. See Dorothy in the Corn Field, Flying Monkey Batallion, Traveling by Lion, Not My Monkeys, and As Sad as That.

John Rea Neill

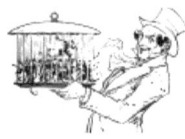

Neill, 1877-1943, was a magazine and children's book illustrator primarily known for illustrating more than forty stories set in the land of Oz, by Frank Baum. See Walk Up to the Door, Whispers, Garden Girl, and Chicken Dance.

Kay Neilsen

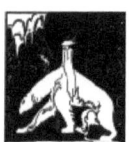

Neilsen, 1886-1957, was a Danish artist who illustrated *East of the Sun and West of the Moon*, Grimm Fairy Tales and worked on Walt Disney's Fantasia. See Cat Moon, Sweet Gifts, and Spring Snow.

About the Author

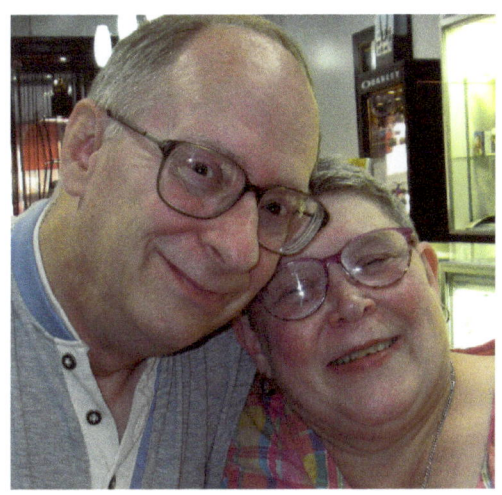

Ellen Anne Eddy is a fiber artist and author who wrote *Thread Magic* and *Thread Magic Garden, The Town of Torper and the Very Vulgar Day Lily,* a series of fiber how-to books, and the *Sight Unseen Series: Tea Room Tales, and The Inverted Cup.* She lives in Galesburg, IL with her husband, Donald Bowers, a greyhound and three cats.

Books by Ellen Anne Eddy

Quilting and Fabric Art

Thread Magic Garden: (2012)

Dragonfly Sky (2009)

Ellen Anne Eddy's Dye Day Workbook (With Lynn Clayton, 2009)

Thread Magic: The Enchanted World of Ellen Anne Eddy (1997)

Ladybug's Garden (2009)

Quick and Easy Machine Binding Methods (2009)

Many Creatures Under Many Skies (2013)

Children's Books

The Town of Torpor and the Very Vulgar Day Lily (2011)

Tigrey Leads the Parade (2009)

Fiction

Sight Unseen Book One: Tea Room Tales (2017)

Sight Unseen Book Two: The Inverted Cup (2018)

Sight Unseen Book Three: The World in Reflection (2018)

For More Information

Check out the TMS Press web site at www.sightunseen2016.wordpress.com

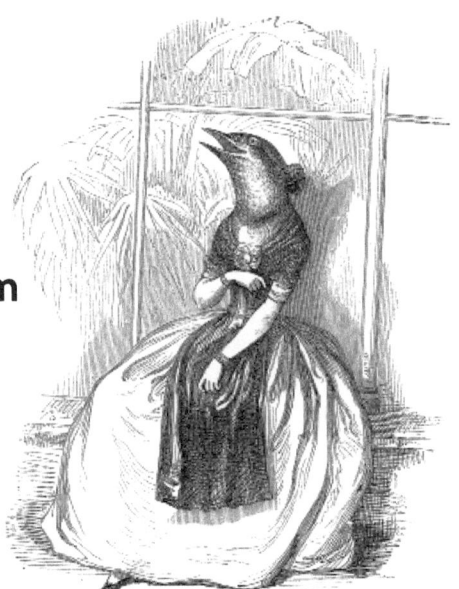

www.ingramcontent.com/pod-product-compliance
Lightning Source LLC
Chambersburg PA
CBHW040408220526
45473CB00004B/1167